The Crafter's Design Library

Florals

Sharon Bennett

D&C

David and Charles

And this one's for you, Dad x

A DAVID & CHARLES BOOK
David & Charles is a subsidiary of F+W (UK) Ltd.,
an F+W Publications Inc. company

First published in the UK in 2005

Distributed in North America
by F+W Publications, Inc.
4700 East Galbraith Road
Cincinnati, OH 45236
1-800-289-0963

A catalogue record for this book is available from the British Library.

ISBN 0 7153 1832 2 hardback
ISBN 0 7153 1833 0 paperback

Printed in Singapare by KHL
for David & Charles
Brunel House   Newton Abbot   Devon

Commissioning Editor Fiona Eaton
Editor Jennifer Proverbs
Senior Designer Lisa Wyman
Production Controller Jen Campbell

Visit our website at www.davidandcharles.co.uk

David & Charles books are available from all good bookshops; alternatively you can contact our
Orderline on (0)1626 334555 or write to us at FREEPOST EX2 110, David & Charles Direct, Newton
Abbot, TQ12 4ZZ (no stamp required UK mainland).

contents

the essential techniques

the templates

Introducing *Floral* art

Flowers are a delight to the senses and a wonderful source of inspiration. Even a single flower can raise the spirits and calm the mind, so it comes as no surprise that they are everywhere, not only in our gardens, hedgerows, parks and botanical gardens but also reproduced on fabrics, home furnishings, wallpapers, greeting cards and just about any other item that can be embellished.

Flowers remind us of the seasons. Think of bluebells, crocuses and daffodils and immediately you are transported to springtime. Roses and lupins conjure up the warm days of summer, while fruits and seed heads signify autumn and bright-leaved poinsettia brings much-needed cheer in winter. These flowers and others are captured in the extensive seasonal collections on pages 28–73 where you'll find a superb range of thoroughly usable crafting motifs that will satisfy the needs of the novice and experienced crafter alike.

The sight of a particular flower can also remind us of a specific location, such as the poppies we associate with cornfields, the dog roses of the hedgerows and the topiary of stately homes, so the seasonal selections are followed by plants that belong to specific places, including ponds and gardens. Following on are flowers associated with special occasions, such as birthdays and weddings (see pages 102–113) and finally you'll find a group of exotics (pages 114–119).

The templates are provided as bold black-and-white images that are easy to trace off and use, and they come in a variety of styles to suit all tastes. You'll find the simplest motifs at the

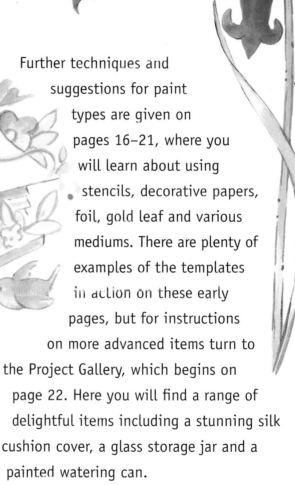

start of each section. All the designs are specifically created so that they are easy to use and suitable for the widest range of applications, but if you need assistance getting started or require advice on adapting and combining designs, you'll find plenty of help on pages 6–15. Here you'll learn how to build a picture out of several motifs, make an all-over design, turn a single motif into a border and more.

Further techniques and suggestions for paint types are given on pages 16–21, where you will learn about using stencils, decorative papers, foil, gold leaf and various mediums. There are plenty of examples of the templates in action on these early pages, but for instructions on more advanced items turn to the Project Gallery, which begins on page 22. Here you will find a range of delightful items including a stunning silk cushion cover, a glass storage jar and a painted watering can.

The designs here can all be found in the templates section of this book. They are versatile designs that could be used for a host of applications. See the Project Gallery, pages 22–25 for further inspiration and advice.

Applying motifs to craft media

The techniques best suited to applying your selected motif to a particular medium depend on the surface you are working with. The following pages offer some simple advice on how to do this for the most popular craft media. Guidance is also given on how to enlarge or reduce the motif to suit your requirements (below) and how to create a stencil (page 11).

Enlarging and reducing a motif

Here are three ways to change the size of a motif to suit your project: the traditional method using a grid, or the modern alternatives of a photocopier or scanner.

Using a grid

The traditional method of enlargement involves using a grid. To begin, use low-tack masking tape to secure tracing paper over the original design. Draw a square or rectangle onto the tracing paper, enclosing the image (see below). Use a ruler to divide up the square or rectangle into rows of equally spaced vertical and horizontal lines. Complex designs should have lines about 1cm (³/₈in) apart; simpler ones can have lines 4cm (1½in) apart.

Now draw a square or rectangle to match your required design size, and draw a grid to correspond with the one you have just drawn over the image, as shown below. You can now begin to re-create the original image by redrawing it, square by square, at the required scale.

Using a photocopier

For fast and accurate results, use a photocopier to enlarge or reduce a motif. To do this, you need to calculate your enlargement percentage. First measure the width of the image you want to end up with. Here, the motif needs to be enlarged to 120mm (4¾in). Measure the width of the original motif, which in this case is 80mm (3¼in). Divide the first measurement by the second to find the percentage by which you need to enlarge the motif, in this instance 150%. (An enlargement must always be more than 100% and a reduction less than 100%).

To photocopy an image onto tracing paper, use tracing paper that is at least 90gsm. When photocopying an image from tracing paper, place the tracing paper onto the glass, and then lay a sheet of white paper on top of it. This will help to produce a sharp copy.

Transferring a motif onto paper, card, wood or fine fabric

A light box makes it easy to trace an image directly onto a piece of paper, thin card or fabric, but if you don't have one it is easy to improvize with household items. Balance a piece of clear plastic across two piles of books or pieces of furniture, and place a table lamp underneath. Place your motif on the plastic and your paper, thin card or fabric on top. Switch on the light and simply trace over the design showing through.

To transfer a design onto wood, thick card or foam, trace the design onto tracing paper using a sharp pencil. Turn the tracing over and redraw on the wrong side with a soft lead pencil. Now turn the tracing over again and use masking tape to secure it right side up onto your chosen surface. Carefully redraw the image – press firmly enough to transfer the motif, but take care not to damage the surface.

Using a scanner

A third way to enlarge or reduce a motif is to scan the original image on a flatbed scanner or to photograph it with a digital camera. Once the image is on your computer you can either adjust the size using image manipulation software or simply alter the percentage of your printout size. If the finished result is larger than the printer's capacity, some software will allow you to tile the image over several sheets of paper, which can then be joined together to form the whole image.

An image manipulation package may also allow you to alter the proportions of a motif, making it wider or narrower, for example. Take care not to distort it beyond recognition, though. Once you are happy with your image, it can be saved to be used again and again.

Transferring a motif onto foil

To emboss foil, simply take the original tracing and secure it to the foil surface. Rest the foil on kitchen paper. Use an embossing tool or an old ballpoint pen that has run out of ink to press down on the tracing, embossing the metal below. Use the same technique on the back of the foil to produce a raised effect.

Transferring a motif onto mirror and ceramic

Trace the motif onto tracing paper, then turn the tracing over and redraw on the wrong side using a chinagraph pencil. A chinagraph produces a waxy line that adheres well to shiny surfaces such as coloured glass, mirrored glass and ceramic. Chinagraphs are prone to blunt quickly, but it doesn't matter if the lines are thick and heavy at this stage. Use masking tape to secure the tracing right side up onto the surface. Carefully redraw with a sharp pencil to transfer the image.

Tracing a motif onto glass and acetate

Roughly cut out the motif and tape it to the underside of the acetate or glass with masking tape. It is helpful to rest glassware on a few sheets of kitchen towel for protection and to stop curved objects from rolling. The image will now show through the clear surface, and you can simply trace along the lines with glass outliner or paint directly onto the surface.

If you want to transfer an image onto opaque glass, or onto a container that is difficult to slip a motif behind, such as a bottle with a narrow neck, follow the instructions on page 7 for transferring a motif onto mirror or ceramic.

Transferring a motif onto curved items

Motifs can be transferred onto rounded items, but will need to be adapted to fit the curves. First trace the motif, redrawing it on the underside (use a chinagraph pencil if the container is ceramic). Make cuts in the template from the edge towards the centre. Lay the motif against the surface so that the cuts slightly overlap or spread open, depending on whether the surface is concave or convex. Tape the motif in place with masking tape and transfer the design by drawing over the lines with a sharp pencil.

Making a template for a straight-sided container

If you wish to apply a continuous motif such as a border to a straight-sided container, make a template of the container first. To do this, slip a piece of tracing paper into a transparent glass container or around an opaque glass or ceramic container. Lay the paper smoothly against the surface and tape in place with masking tape. Mark the position of the upper edge of the container with a pencil. Now mark the position of the overlapping ends of the paper or mark each side of the handle on a mug, cup or jug.

Remove the tracing and join the overlap marks, if you have made these. Measure down from the upper edge and mark the upper limit of the band or border on the template. Cut out the template and slip it into or around the container again to check the fit. Transfer your chosen template onto the tracing paper, then onto the container.

Making a template for a plate

1 Cut a square of tracing paper slightly larger than the diameter of the plate. Make a straight cut from one edge to the centre of the paper. Place the paper centrally on the plate or saucer and tape one cut edge across the rim. Roughly cut out a circle from the centre of the paper to help it lie flat. Smooth the paper around the rim and tape in place, overlapping the cut edges. Mark the position of the overlap on the paper.

2 Turn the plate over and draw around the circumference onto the underside of the tracing paper. Remove the paper, then measure the depth of the plate rim and mark it on the paper by measuring in from the circumference. Join the marks with a curved line.

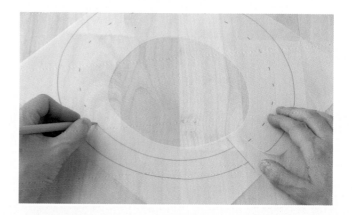

Transferring a motif onto fabric

If fabric is lightweight and pale in colour, it may be possible to trace the motif simply by laying the fabric on top. If the fabric is dark or thick, it may help to use a light box. Place the motif under the fabric on the surface of the light box (see page 7 for information on constructing a home light box). As the light shines up through the motif and fabric you should be able to see the design lines, ready for tracing.

Alternatively, place a piece of dressmaker's carbon paper face down on the fabric and tape the motif on top with masking tape. Trace the design with a sharp pencil to transfer it onto the fabric as shown below. The marks made by the carbon are easily wiped away.

Transferring a motif onto a knitting chart

Use knitting-chart paper rather than ordinary graph paper to chart a knitting design. (Knitted stitches are wider than they are tall and knitting chart paper is sized accordingly.) Transfer the motif straight onto the knitting graph paper (see page 7 for advice on transferring onto paper). Each square on the graph paper represents a stitch. Make sure that you are happy with the number of squares in the motif, as this dictates the number of stitches in your design, and ultimately the design size. Fill in the applicable squares on the chart using appropriate coloured pens or pencils.

Use the finished chart in conjunction with a knitting pattern. Read the chart from right to left for a knit row and from left to right for a purl row. The motif can also be worked on a ready-knitted item with Swiss darning.

Transferring a motif onto needlepoint canvas and cross stitch fabric

Designs on needlepoint canvas and cross stitch fabric can be worked either by referring to the design on a chart, or by transferring the image to the material and stitching over it.

To transfer the motif onto a chart

Transfer the motif straight onto graph paper (see page 7 for advice on transferring onto paper). Each square on the graph paper represents a square of canvas mesh or Aida cross stitch fabric. Colour in the squares that the motif lines cross with coloured pencils or pens. You may want to make half stitches where the motif outline runs through a box. Mark the centre of the design along a vertical and horizontal line (see right) and mark the centre of the fabric lengthways and widthways with tacking stitches.

To transfer the motif directly onto canvas or fabric

With an open-weave canvas or pale fabric it is possible to trace the design directly onto the canvas or fabric. First, mark a small cross centrally on the motif and on the material. On a lightbox (see page 7), place the material on top of the motif, aligning the crosses. Tape in position and trace the image with a waterproof pen. Alternatively, use dressmaker's carbon paper to transfer the design, as explained in transferring a motif onto fabric, opposite.

Making a stencil

Tape a piece of tracing paper over the motif to be adapted into a stencil. Redraw the image, thickening the lines and creating 'bridges' between the sections to be cut out. You may find it helpful to shade in the areas to be cut out. Lay a piece of carbon paper, ink side down, on a stencil sheet, place the tracing on top, right side up, and tape in place. Redraw the design to transfer it to the stencil sheet. Finally, lay the stencil sheet on a cutting mat and carefully cut out the stencil with a craft knife, always drawing the sharp edge of the blade away from you.

Building a picture

Although you can use the templates in this book exactly as they are, a lot of fun is to be had simply messing around with them, taking sections out, adding bits in, combining different motifs and so on. You can do this endlessly, making your library of templates never-ending as your ideas become new images.

Changing dimensions

Often you want a design to fit a specific space, but you may find that a simple enlargement or reduction on a photocopier doesn't quite work. All is not lost – just make your plants grown taller or sprout at the sides for added width. Here more stem sections and leaves make the flowers from page 78 higher. If the plant is too big, just do some selective pruning.

Making a bouquet

Take some of your favourite leaf and flower shapes and assemble them into a bouquet, repeating the same motifs as many times as necessary. This could be a geometrical design like the one shown, which would suit many applications, or you could build a realistic bouquet of seasonal flowers and place them in a vase or pot. (See page 75 for these motifs.)

Recombining

Pull each design apart in your mind and decide if you could create a more interesting image by moving the elements and perhaps adding part of a different design. Here the leaves have been separated from the stem of the sprig on page 75 and a flower inserted in the middle (from the paisley design on the same page) to create a whole new look.

Building borders

Don't neglect the edges of your design. There are a number of borders in this book, but you can also create your own using just about any design and a little imagination. Here an elegant leaf shape (page 75) has been flipped and repeated with single, smaller leaves (from the same page) placed in the gaps. This would make a great all-over background in a very light colour.

If you want to send a message or quote a poem, it can look eye-catching to create a design that is made up solely of a frame, leaving the centre free for your words.

Taking it further

Don't just stop at your first idea. You may be able to create lots of good designs out of one simple shape. Here a basic fan shape (page 75) has been repeated and rotated six times to make a flower. Add a smaller version of the same design in a different colour and it makes a pretty centre. You could also repeat the same simple design to make an attractive border. The creative possibilities are endless.

Doing a flip

A repeat image makes an impressive background or border when it is flipped or rotated for a symmetrical effect. Here the campion silhouette design from page 98 (shown below repeated as a mirror image) is used in two arrangements (right) for dramatically different results. This would be great on fabrics.

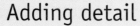

Adding detail

Working a design up into something more complex takes a little work, but it doesn't have to be a challenge. For example, the simple dog rose with heart-shaped petals from page 45 gets a new centre by repeating the same design smaller and adding a few extra loops. Likewise the petals have been repeated smaller for a more elaborate effect. A few extra leaves and tendrils complete the look.

Containing a design

Using frames and borders to hold an image is a very useful device, particularly with techniques such as glass or fabric painting when you may wish to work just a small area. You can draw short lines from the frame to touch the central motif to 'secure' it and create little compartments that you can colour individually, if desired. Here, the border from the vase on page 110 has been simplified and combined with the daffodils from page 33 to show how such a border can be adapted.

Repeating patterns

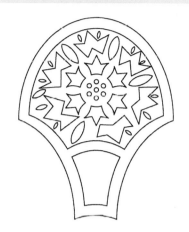

A number of templates can be repeated to make borders or all-over patterns without any further adaptation, like this pretty little shape (page 43), reminiscent of an Arab tile, which locks into itself brilliantly. It works well on a large scale as an all-over pattern, perhaps as a background for scrap booking, but would also make an excellent border if reduced in size.

To get an idea of how a motif will look when repeated or rotated, trace or photocopy it several times and cut it out. Then arrange the copies on a fresh sheet of paper and move them about until you like the effect. If necessary, copy and cut out other motifs to fill the gaps.

Using silhouettes

The black silhouette templates make excellent stencils or stamps or can be traced and painted for a bold effect. But you don't have to use them like this. Here the honeysuckle from page 56 has been reduced and repeated to make a striking border that has also been rotated and used as a 'positive'.

This idea can be turned around – you can make any of the positive images at the back of the book into silhouettes for a bold effect that can look radically different from the original.

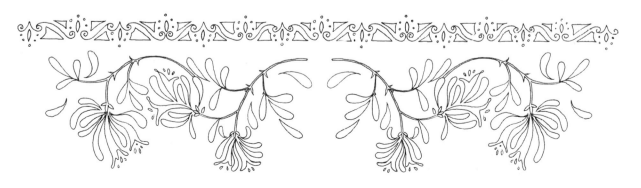

Techniques and mediums

Flowers are such beautiful subjects that they look great in practically any medium and even as simple line drawings. The problem is narrowing down your options. Here is just a selection to get your fingers twitching into action.

Metal and foil

Tracing over a design onto metal or foil sheets with an embossing tool will produced a depressed line on the side that is uppermost and a raised line on the underneath. Even the simplest designs, such as this teapot from page 106, will look great on cards or labels and they can be painted for further embellishment, if desired.

If you don't have an embossing tool, an old trick is to use a worn-out biro instead to emboss foil or paper. Other tools can be used too, such as a large tapestry needle, wooden skewer or the end of a paintbrush.

Stencils

Stencils are a great means of transferring a design to just about any surface from paper or fabric to ceramics, glass or terracotta and they come into their own when you want to use the same design several times over. Simply trace the design onto stencil film or acetate and cut out carefully with a sharp craft knife or hot stencil iron. For a soft, blended effect use a proper stencil brush and take off the excess paint on scrap paper each time you reload your brush so you are only applying a little colour at a time. This motif can be found on page 52.

If you are using a stencil several times in a row, for example to make an all-over design, paint can build up around the cutout and smear the design. To avoid this give the stencil a quick rub round with a lint-free cloth after each use.

Decorative papers

There are endless varieties of papers available to the crafter that can be used in a host of different ways. You can fold them or curl them for a three-dimensional effect, or you can simply tear them or cut them and stick in place as I did here, cutting out each element of the design in a different paper. Open up further decorative possibilities by using shaped cutters and scissors as I did on the large heart in each example. You'll find this motif on page 104.

Fabric paints

You can paint or dye any natural material and some synthetics for a variety of lovely effects provided you use the right product for that particular fibre. Cottons and linens can be painted with fabric paints, pens, crayons or sprays but silk is in a category all of its own. Silk paints spread over the fabric with amazing speed and need to be contained by a raised outline drawing in gutta that defines each colour area. This works particularly well with floral designs, and the fabric can be used for cards or turned into attractive handkerchiefs, cushions, scarves, ties, costumes or even curtains. The design shown here is on page 33.

Découpage

Découpage is a lovely craft that involves cutting out and sticking down paper motifs, often cut from wrapping paper. Experiment with other papers, avoiding very thick types, which are the most difficult to finish effectively (see the tip). Try tracing suitable designs, such as this rose ball (page 108), onto paper, painting them and then colour photocopying them onto thin paper. Then all you have to do is cut them out and stick them to a painted item. Apply several protective coats of varnish to finish.

Thin papers, such as tissue paper work best for découpage and you can photocopy onto it for some lovely results.

Reversing out

Designs with striking outlines can be used 'reversed out' from a coloured background for a dramatic effect, as on this green and gold card. Use a solid colour to paint the background around the design or use a paint technique, such as stippling. I dabbed off the excess paint before it dried for an antiqued look. If desired you can reinforce the shape with white paint. On silk you can reverse out by applying clear gutta to the design lines and then painting around the shapes instead of in them. On paper or ceramic you can use masking fluid as on the pink jug, page 22.

See page 101 for this design.

The design areas cut from stencils make great masks for reversing out. Simply position on the paper and sponge paint around them. When the paint is nearly dry, lift off the masks to reveal the finished design.

Tonal images

Using just one colour in a design emphasizes shape and form. In watercolour or acrylic you can do this by building up layers of a single wash or by diluting the wash to make a lighter and lighter tint. With drawing tools such as coloured pencils you may need to purchase two or three shades of the same colour. This technique works really well with geometrical designs, as shown, but also in figurative work, as can be seen on willow-pattern plates and other ceramics, for example. See pages 43 and 83 for these motifs.

Cerne relief and glitter glue

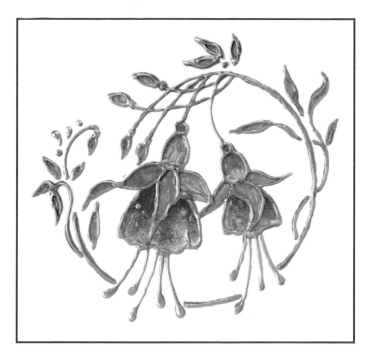

Cerne relief comes in a tube with a long nozzle and is used like gutta except that it is applied to paper to create a raised outline. It is available in all sorts of colours, although gold is a favourite for creating a lavish, elegant look as in the fuchsia design here (see page 53). Outliners are also manufactured to use on porcelain or glass, although these need baking to make them permanent. Glitter glues are excellent for adding highlights and children love them.

Cerne relief can be used to make lovely 'brailed' cards and gift tags. You can use it to write messages too, and children will love tracing over their names with a finger.

Choosing a medium

If you are painting on ceramics or fabrics your choice of medium is limited to what is specifically designed for that product, but when working on paper or card there are many ranges at your disposal. Here are some of the most versatile and readily available.

Metallic and pearlized paints

Metallic and pearlized paints can be used on their own or as highlights on work produced with other paints or mediums. Metallics add a super shiny look that can be really eye catching while iridescent colours add a more subtle sheen that only shows up when the light catches them.

Pearlized colours show up best when applied on top of a dark background as on the flowers shown here.

Metallic leaf

Gold and silver leaf used to be the province of the professionals, but with the introduction of imitation metallic leaf we can now all use it. Leaf is available in several metallic finishes and is easy to apply. You simply paint size (special glue) over the area to be covered, press on the thin foil and rub it down, then brush away the excess. If there are gaps, just apply more size and foil until the whole area is covered. It looks very stylish and expensive.

Gold leaf works well as a highlight or for a name or number on a card and it looks wonderful brushed over three-dimensional objects.

Crayons and pencils

Crayons and coloured pencils are not just tools for the very young. You can make some excellent, soft broken lines with these, and some are watersoluble so they can be washed with water to blend and smudge like watercolours, as you can see in the violet and primrose design here, adapted from the design on page 41.

Watercolour and ink

Watercolour is one of the most popular mediums. Use proprietary watercolour paper and stretch it to avoid warping or buy pads that are pre-stretched. Apply the colour in light, thin washes to build up colour gently, as on the pea and sweet pea image here (see page 56), or wash on plenty of strong colour for drama. Acrylic inks can be applied with brushes in the same way and come in lovely vibrant colours. Either medium can be combined with pen and waterproof ink outlines, as on the acorn design here (see page 89).

Keep colours very light to start with and build up slowly because with watercolour you can add darker tones but you can't lighten what is already there.

Project gallery

Just about any item can be decorated with floral motifs from a chest of drawers to a glass jar and even a watering can. You'll find plenty of ideas here to get you started, which you can copy, re-create using different motifs or simply use as inspiration for your own ideas.

rose jug

This beautiful country-look jug utilizes part of the leafy design from page 85. The design was enlarged, traced onto a white ceramic jug and then painted with masking fluid. Once the fluid was completely dry, it was covered with pale pink heat-set paint using a stencil brush in a dabbing motion. When the paint was dry the masking fluid was rubbed away.

topiary plant pot

Transform a standard terracotta pot with any of the designs in this book. Here the pot was decorated with a stencil of the topiary tree from page 80. The colours are greens and apricots, which complement the warm brown of the pot but you could try adding your own third colour to suit the surroundings or the plant. Lemon would work well or turquoise. Use exterior paints to make this weather proof.

daisy stationery

Keep in touch and impress your friends with this personal set of stationery. It's a simple linocut, which is thought of as an old-fashioned method but boy does it produce some fantastic prints. The lino was cut into the shape of the daisy from page 94 and used to print onto cards and envelopes. You can keep printing off these images if you clean the lino well between each use and no two prints will ever be the same, so you'll be making some brilliant one offs.

Try putting two colours on the roller when you ink up. Where they meet they will blend to create a third colour for a lovely effect.

Always think about the insides of you items and whether or not these can be seen. Sometimes it is wise to paint the inside as far as the eye can see.

flower garden

Make gardening a joy with this super little matching set. These items were first primed then painted with a pale yellow, pink and green background. The clematis from the summer section (page 57) was added and the border from page 83. Colours have been kept pale but bright and limited to tones of greens, pinks and yellows. Varnish would make these accessories practical and durable.

blackberry chest

Transform old, battered furniture with paint. This chest was first painted green and cream using thick paint applied roughly for a distressed look. Then the blackberry motif and flower from page 96 were hand painted onto the front. On the sides a silhouette design from the same page was given an amber tone, which changes from dark to light for added depth.

It demonstrates that silhouettes can be any colour. If preferred, découpage or stencilling would also work well.

If the wood is in fairly good order and hasn't been painted before you can use stain instead of paint to allow wood grain to show through.

silk tulip cushion

There's nothing quite like finishing a room with a unique cushion. Here gold gutta was used for the outlines and silk paints were applied in soft colours to complement the tulips from page 31. The design has been enlarged to sit nicely in the centre and a border from page 120 placed around the edge. If a pillow seems too large a project for you to start with, make a smaller design for a card or even a handkerchief.

lavender candles

These candles are painted with the lavender stem from page 50 at varying heights. You can take these all round the candle or just have one at the front. Paints allow freedom to achieve detail and are quick and easy to use, but if preferred you can decorate candles with designs cut from thin sheets of wax or use outliner.

poppy storage jar

A gorgeous effect was created on this clear glass jar by using a pewter-coloured outliner to reproduce the poppy design from page 92 in panels on the sides. Once dry, the panels were filled in with glass paints and baked to make the jar practical.

glittering tray

Breakfast in bed is even more special with a tray like this, created on a wooden or papier-mâchè blank. Prepare the surface with a coat of primer, then apply your background – in this case blue acrylic. The image of scabious from page 47 was used in the centre and then partly repeated at intervals around the edge. An ornate border of triangles was added and glitter glue used to pick out details. This type of surface is also excellent for découpage (see page 18).

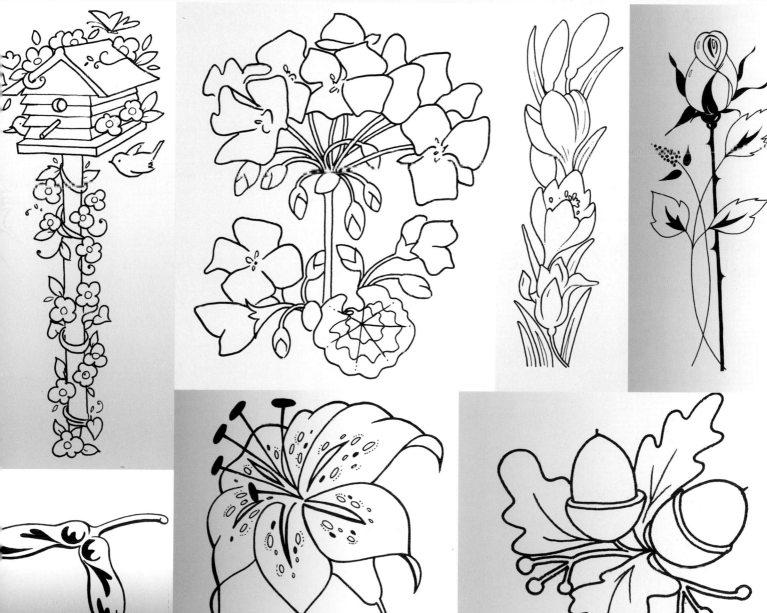

the
templates

Spring

This is the season of regeneration when new life bursts into the baron landscapes of winter bringing cheer and the hope of warm days ahead. It is an exciting season when we see the first glimpses of round sticky buds and new shoots followed by the heads of those early bright bulbs, the crocuses.

Spring images are widely used in crafting. Often shapes are simple but colours are bright and vibrant with a fresh, clean note. We see the rich pinks of the crocuses, the cheerful yellows of daffodils and the myriad bright colours of tulips. These three spring favourites begin the collection in this chapter, followed by lovely lily-of-the-valley, elegant irises, hyacinths and shrubs such as magnolia, peonies and lilac. The collection concludes with those delicate beauties, violets and primroses, which always seem to be in flower at Easter time.

To complement your floral motifs you'll find some rabbits and lambs skipping across the pages, with a ladybird and nesting baby birds. These images will add to the spring flavour of your designs.

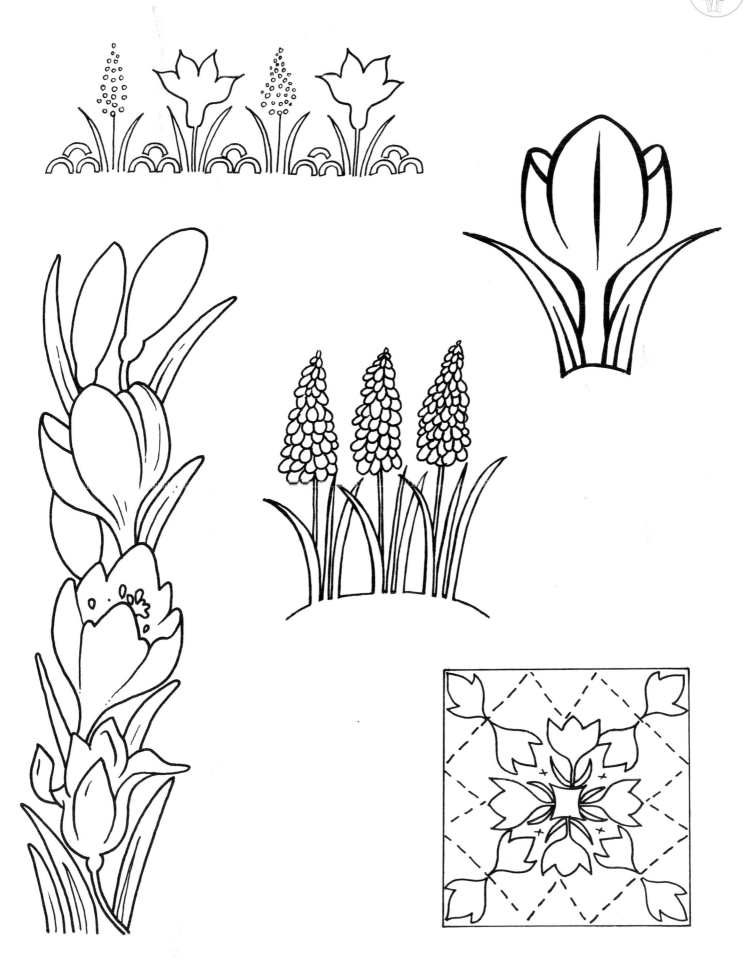

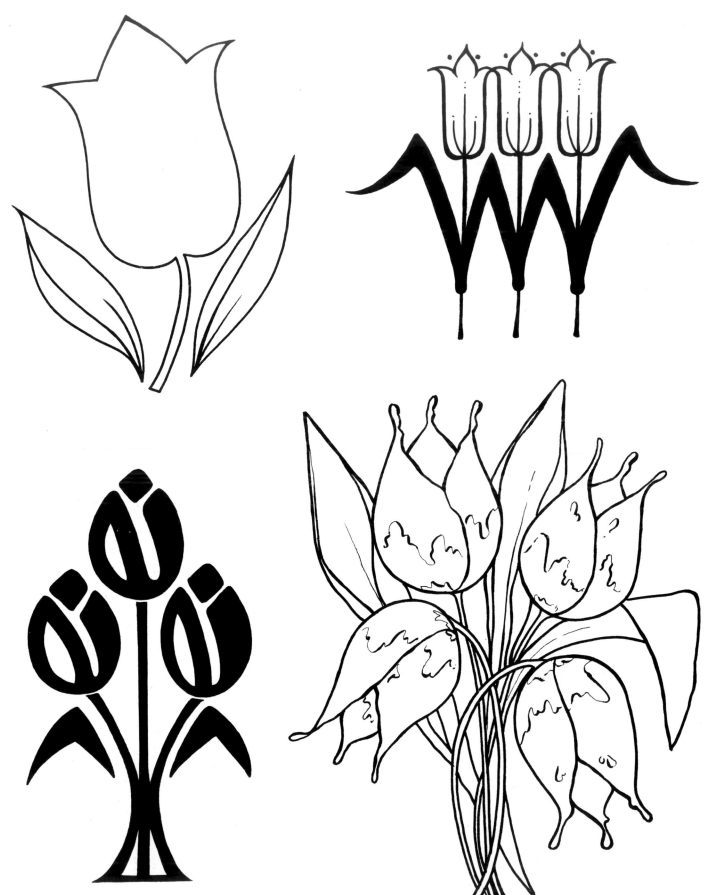

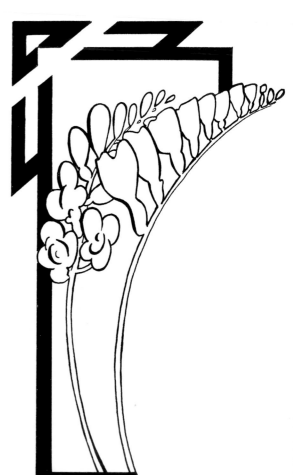

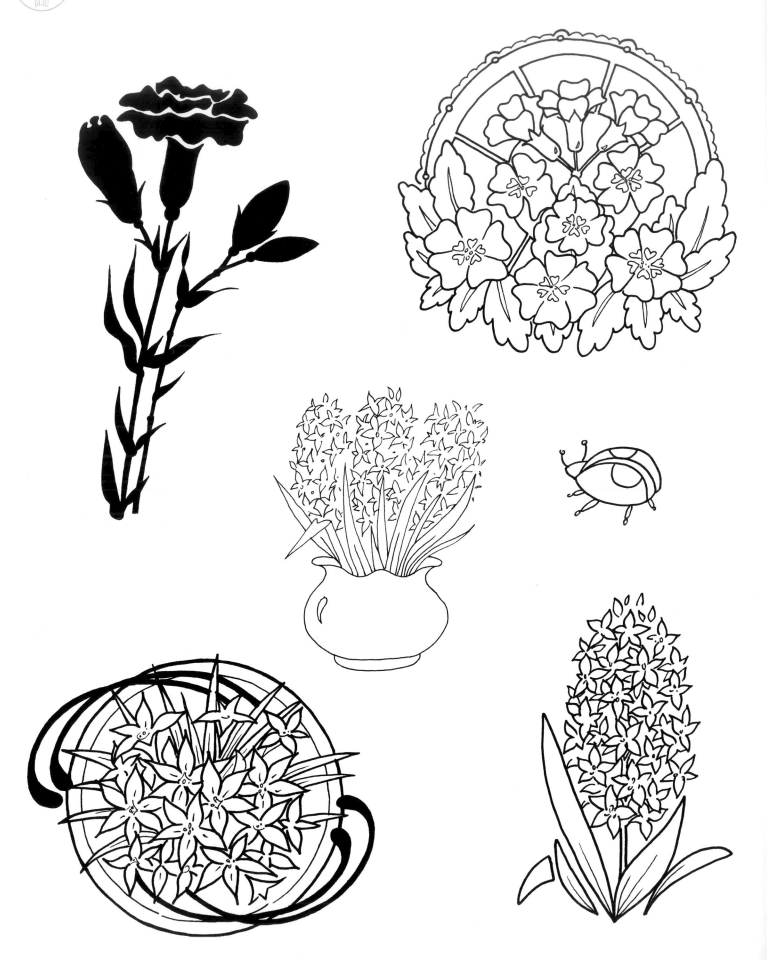

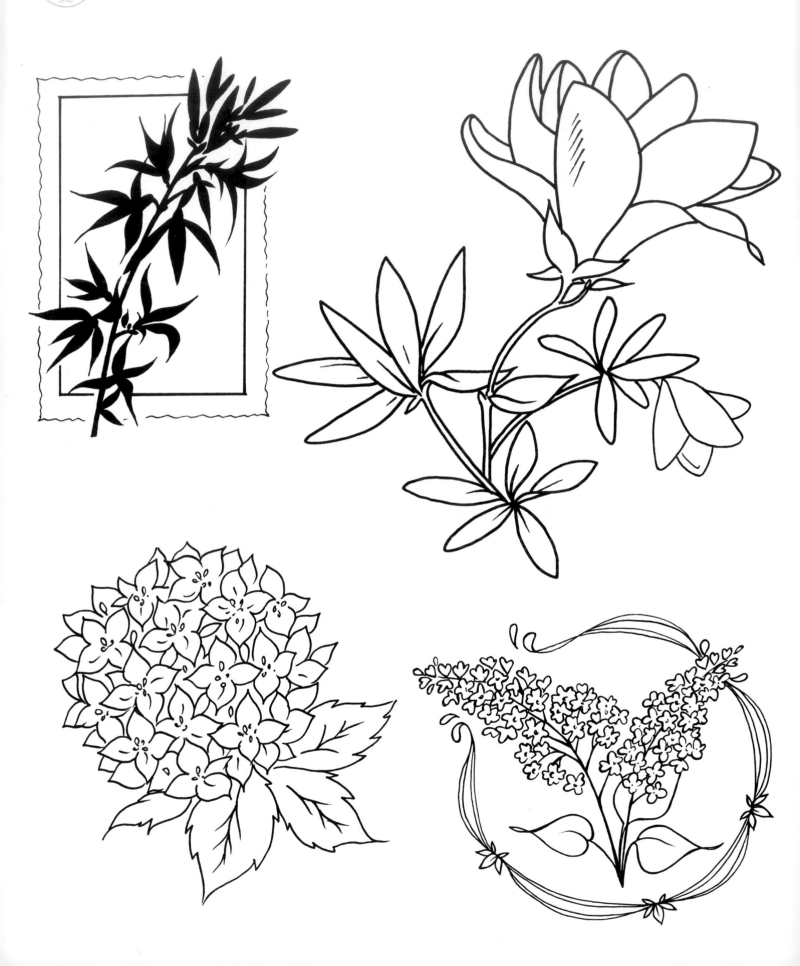

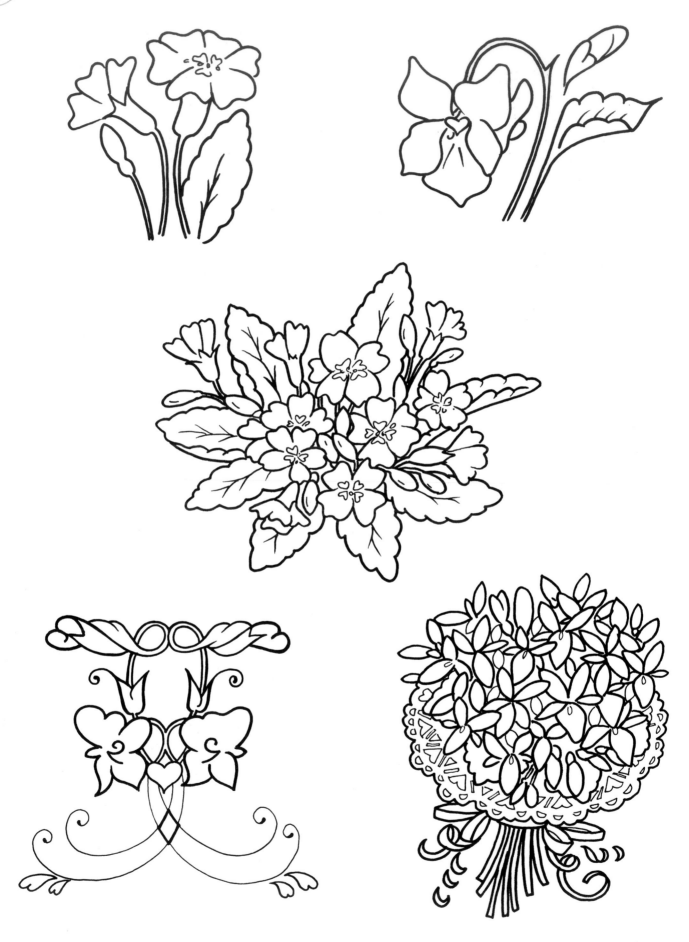

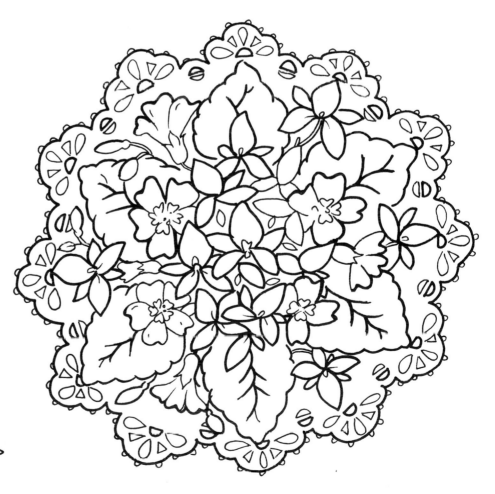

Summer

It is now that flowers are at their most glorious, surrounding us with colour and sweet perfume. This is a time to soak up the beauty of Nature in our gardens or the countryside; a time for picnics and walks, outdoor games and other activities or simply an opportunity to stretch out and relax in the sun.

Starting with some simple, stylized images, which are highly versatile and usable, the templates in this section move on to include sunflowers and lilies, roses, sweet Williams, pinks, fuchsias and more, with spring delphiniums, gladioli and hollyhocks and pendulous wisteria along with other climbers such as clematis, honeysuckle and sweet peas. All these lend themselves beautifully to a host of crafting projects and the twist and turn of tendrils and leafy branches allow artistic licence to come into its own.

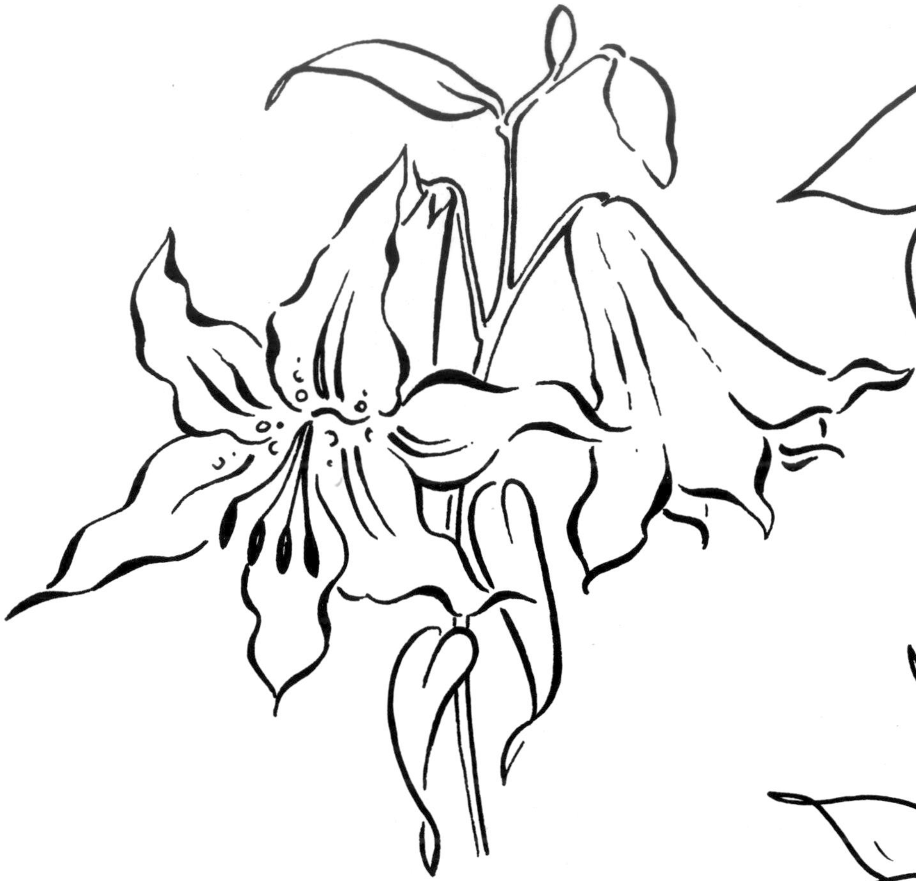

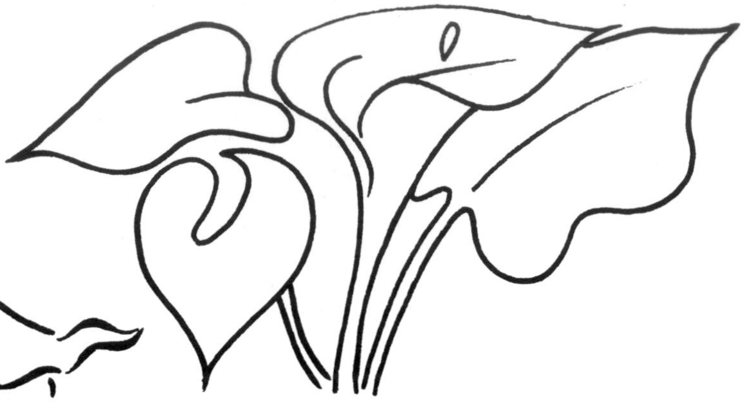

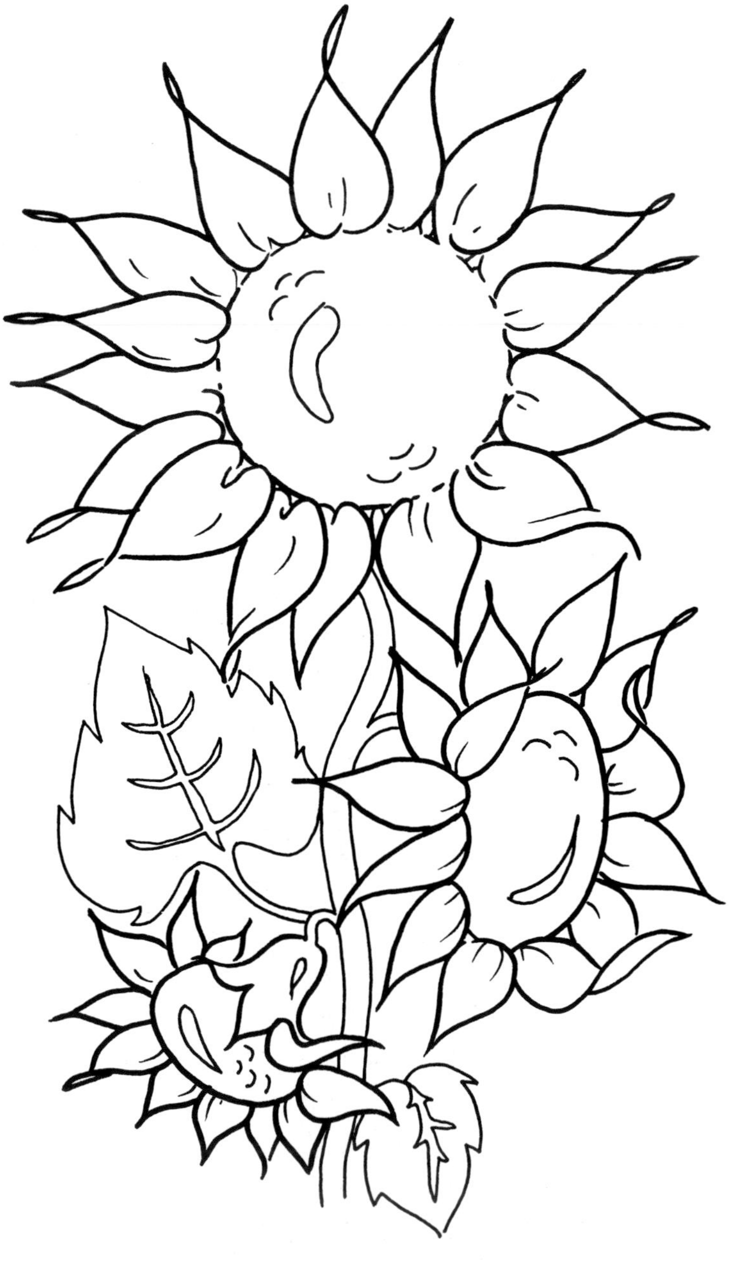

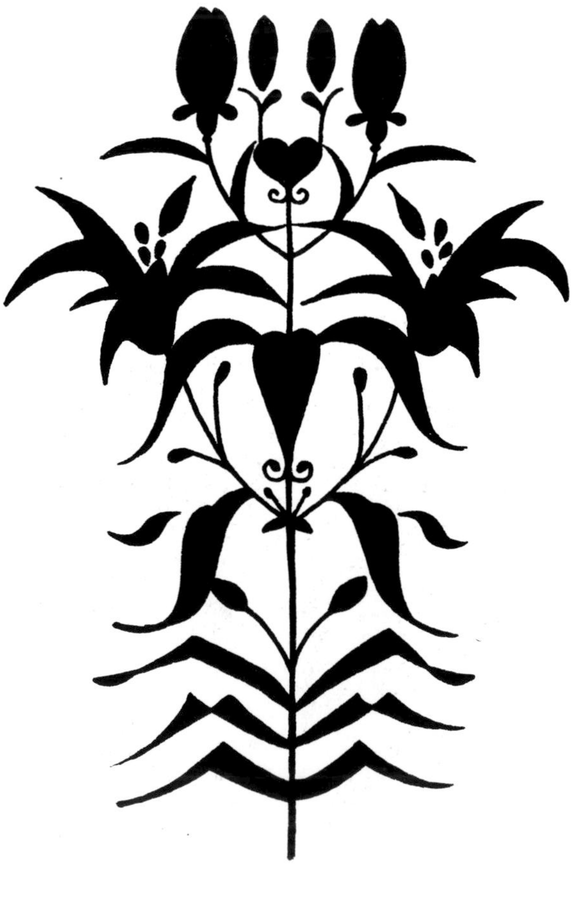

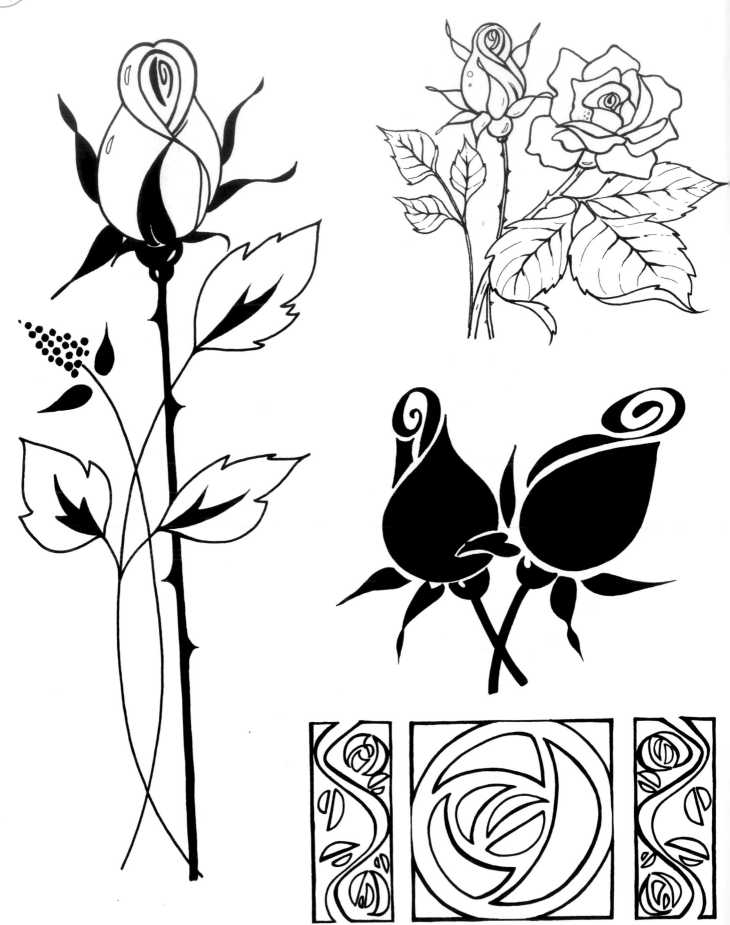

Autumn

A rich feast of reds, oranges, ochres and golds awaits us in autumn, blending with the greens of those leaves that haven't yet turned colour. Highlights come from the reds and purples of berries and from the greys, whites and browns of seed heads. This is the season of harvest but there are still some flowers around, such as dahlias, chrysanthemums and asters, which seem more beautiful in the flattering golden light of the long evenings.

Bronze and copper make excellent additions to your palette of colours, emphasizing the richness of the season and adding a glorious sheen. Combine these with oranges, reds and greens to provide a feast for the eye.

The motifs begin with seeds and leaves, moving on to fruits and then flowers, and scattered over the pages are some birds and forest animals that we particularly associate with autumn, such as the squirrel and hedgehog, to add detail to your work.

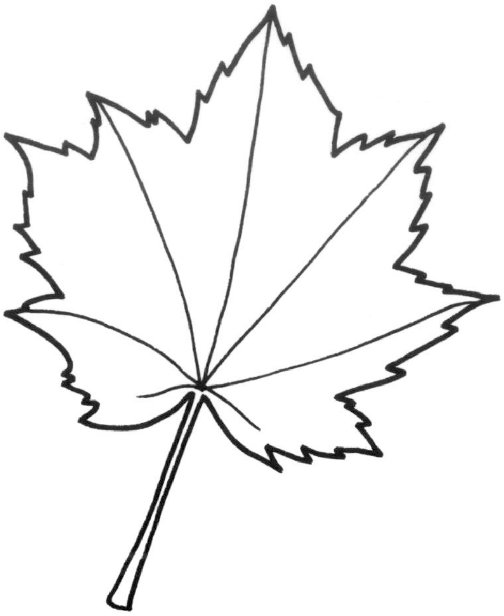

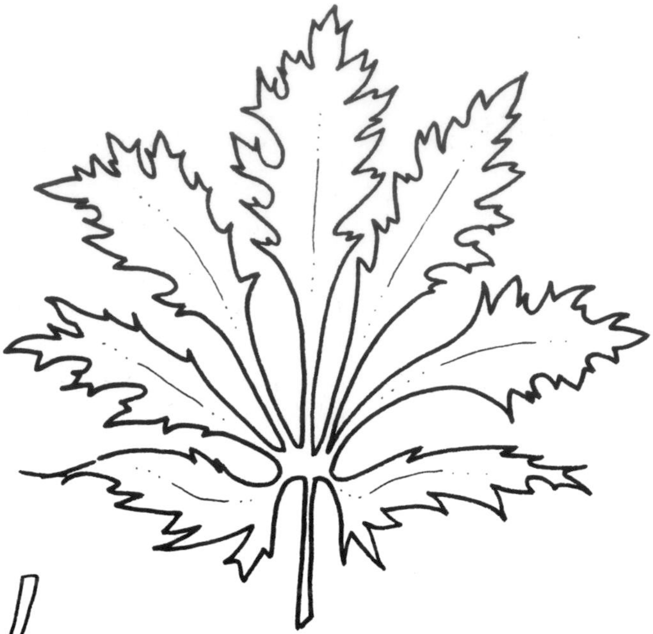

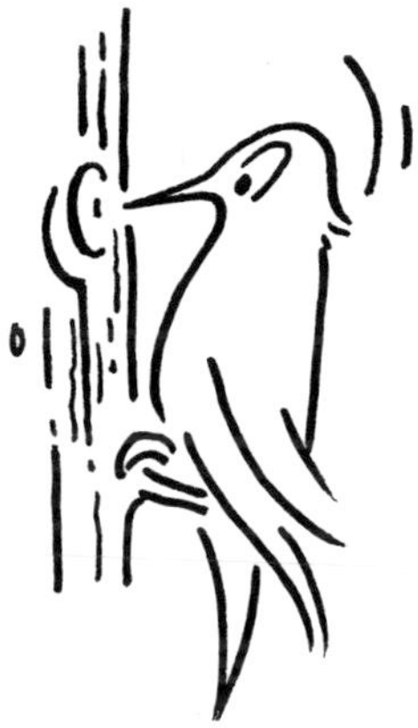

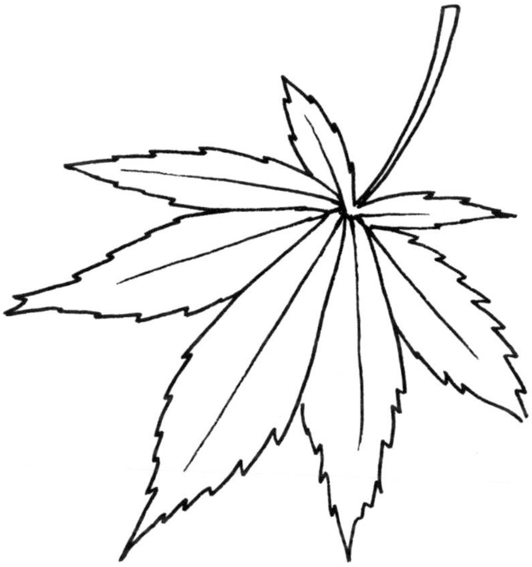

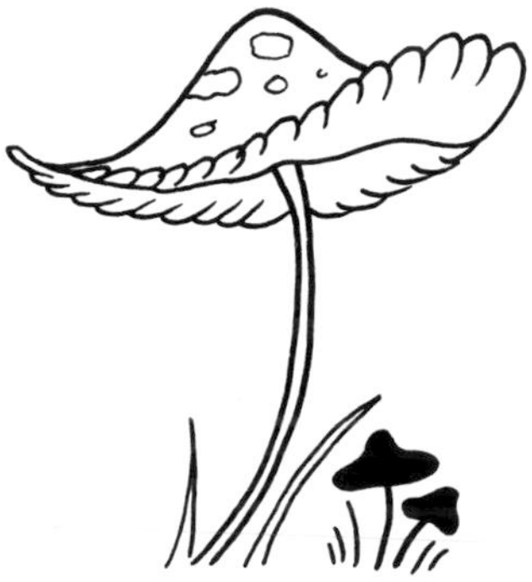

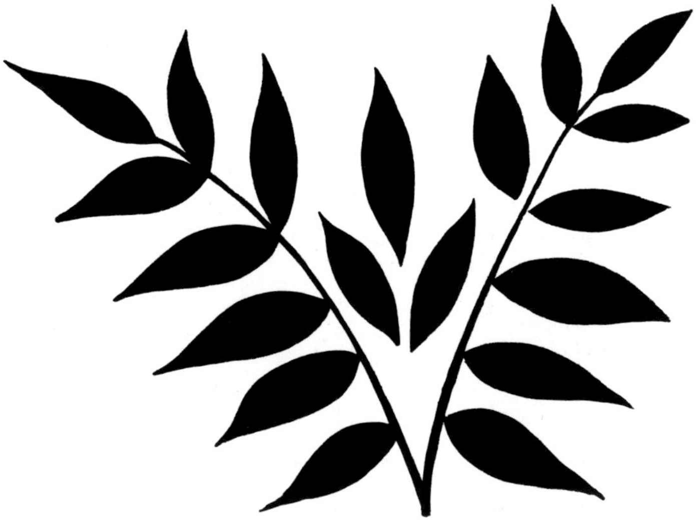

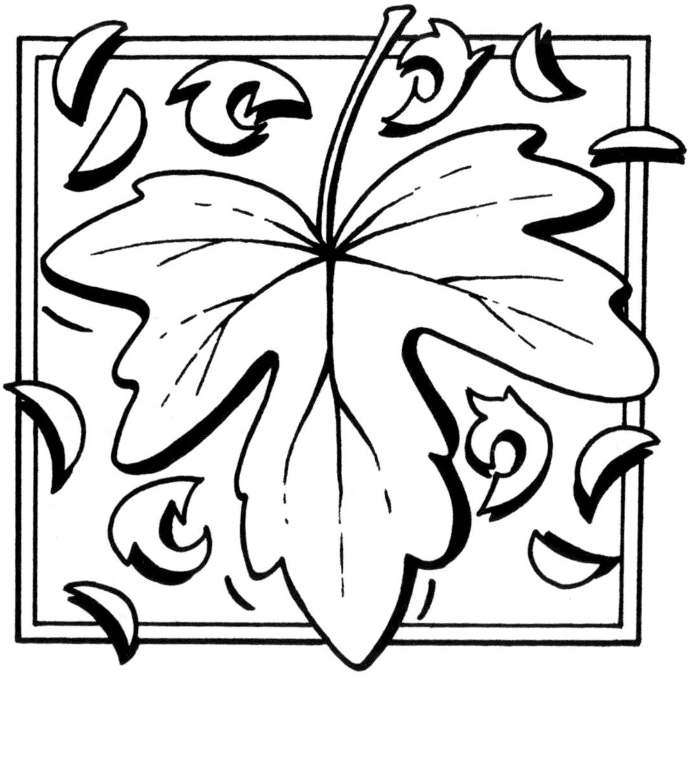

Winter

This icy season presents us with dramatic and sometimes surprisingly colourful images – sharp and crisp, the low sun gives us spectacular pink sunsets. Leaves have all but disappeared from the trees, leaving silhouettes of twisted branches against gradated skies. Snow drifts over the landscape and lies heavy on branches, and ice twinkles like stars on windows, rocks and trees.

Indoors pots of striking amaryllis and bright-leaved poinsettias add festive cheer while outside we have winter aconites and sweet-smelling winter jasmine, and there are still some colourful berries and evergreens including holly, ivy and mistletoe. These can be brought indoors in wreaths or table arrangements or hung outside to bring cheer to visitors. As early as the beginning of January snowdrops begin to peep out from under the leaves as harbingers of spring.

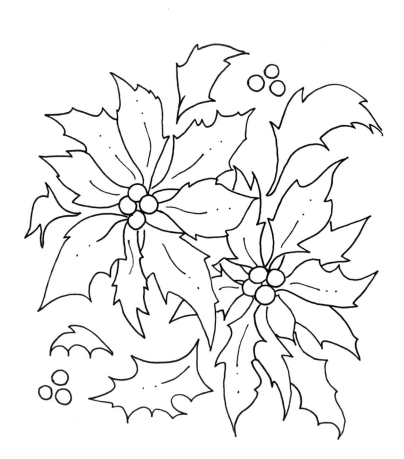

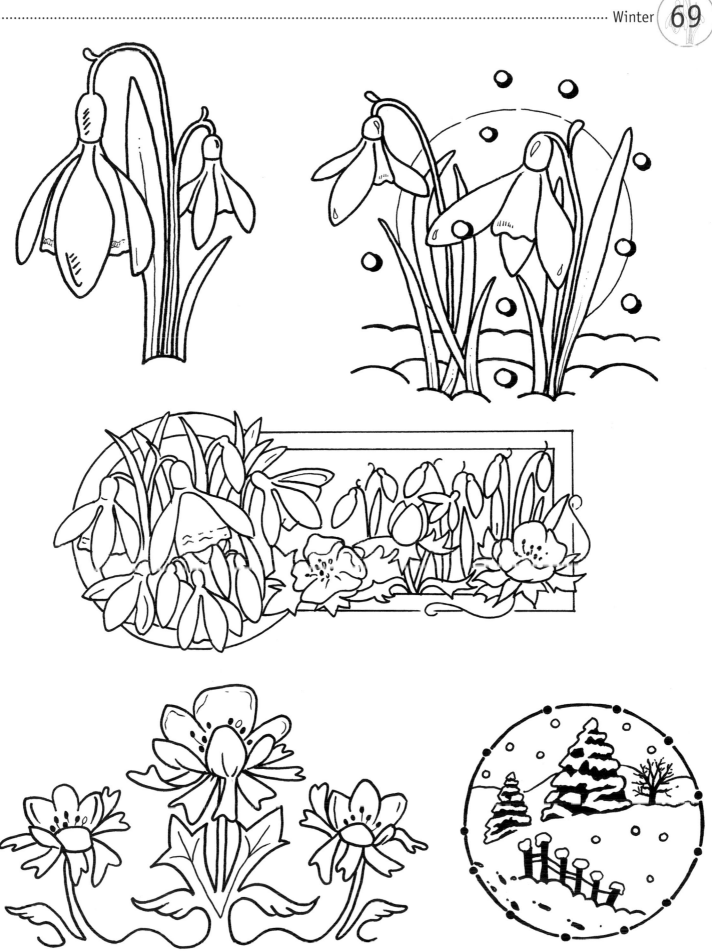

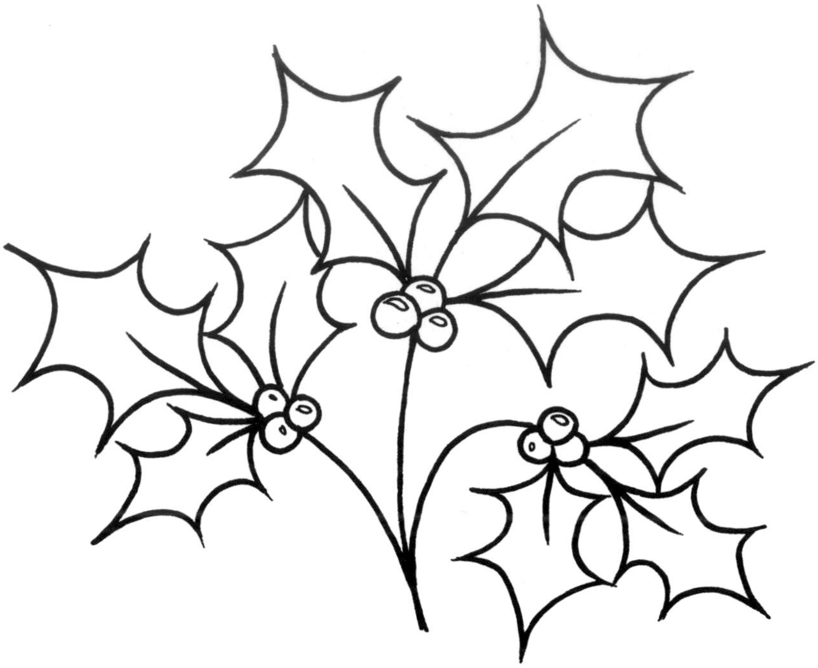

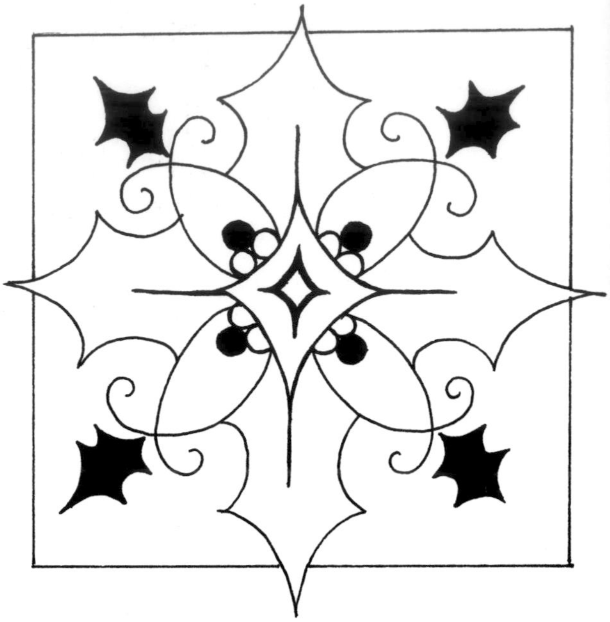

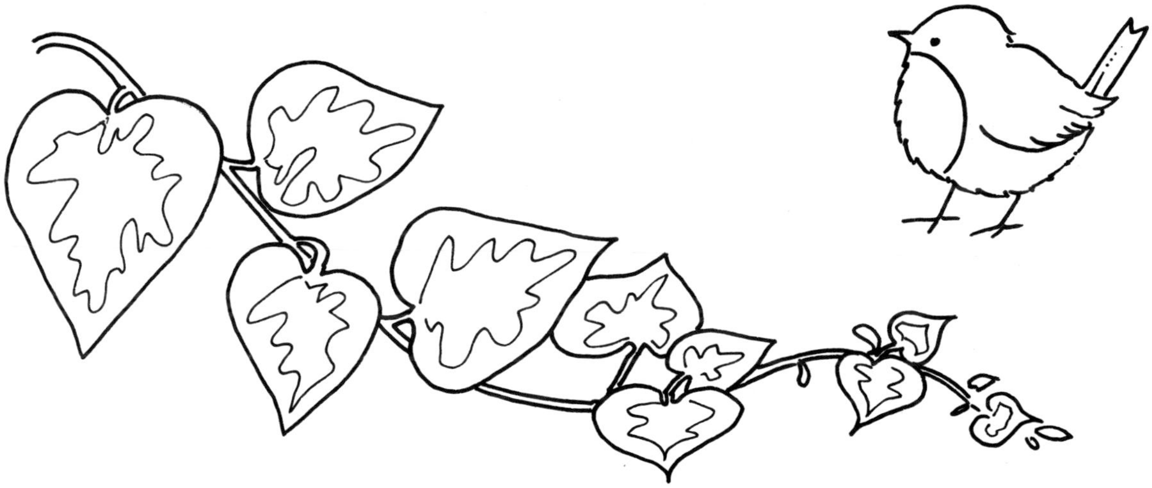

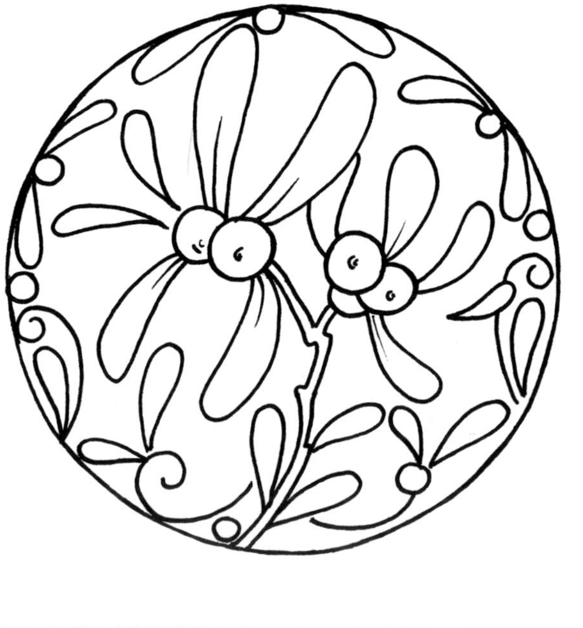

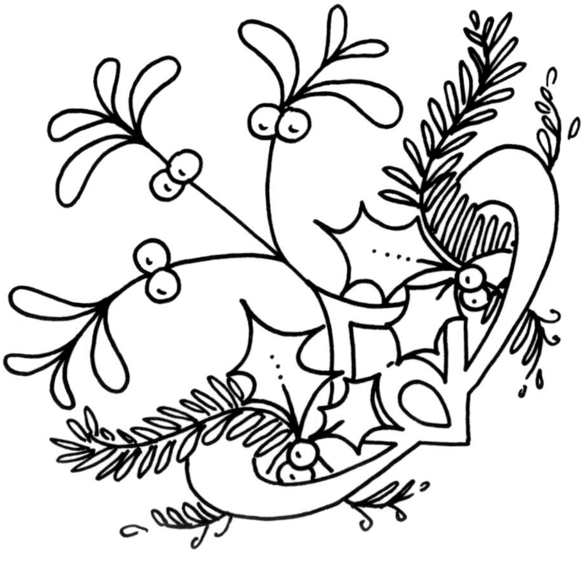

Garden

Gardening as we know it was once the pastime of the rich, who would employ landscape designers and a team to attend to the day-to-day business of potting, planting and pruning. Today many of us like to indulge in gardening, even if our patch comprises pots and hanging baskets in a yard or patio, and we dream of an idyllic garden of our own.

For many people the cottage garden is the ideal, with rose-entwined arches, wicket gates and a pretty pond, so many cottage-style images are included here, along with a variety of flower-filled pots and tubs. Topiary is enjoying a revival, so there are also several examples here and a useful collection of borders and frames to help you complete your designs. We begin, though, with a very simple selection of leaf and flower shapes that you can combine to create your own designs (see pages 12–13 for some examples).

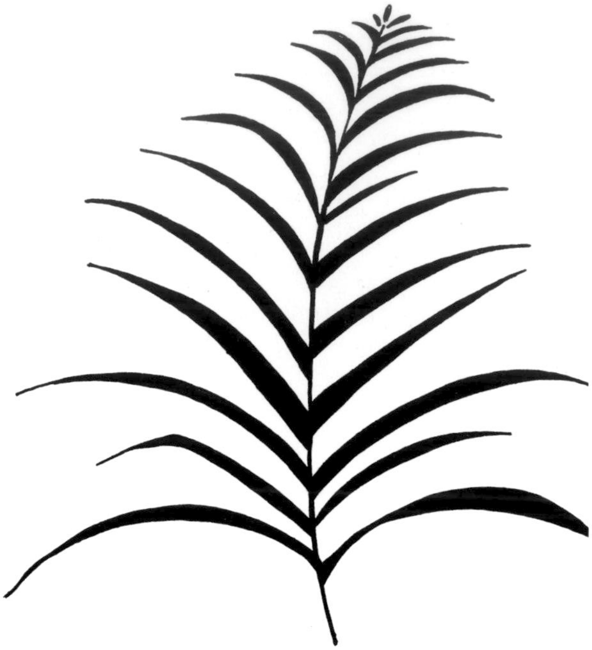

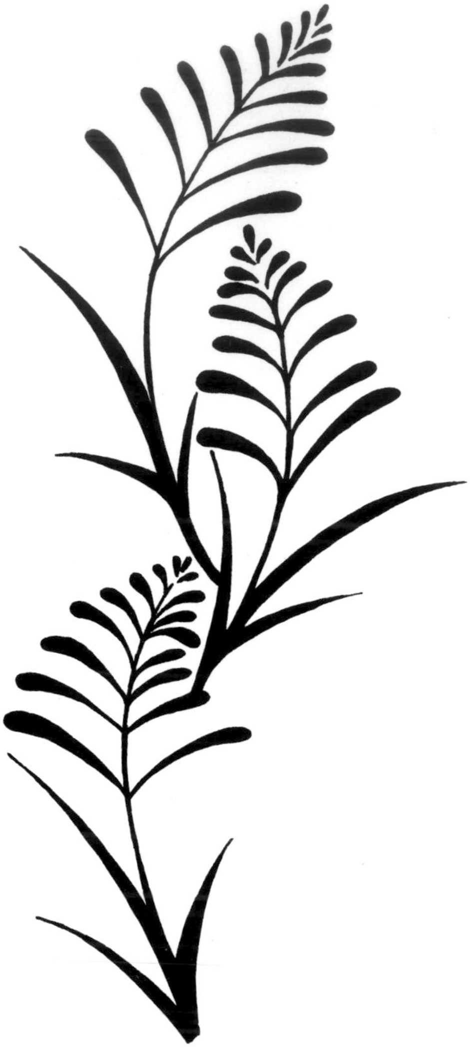

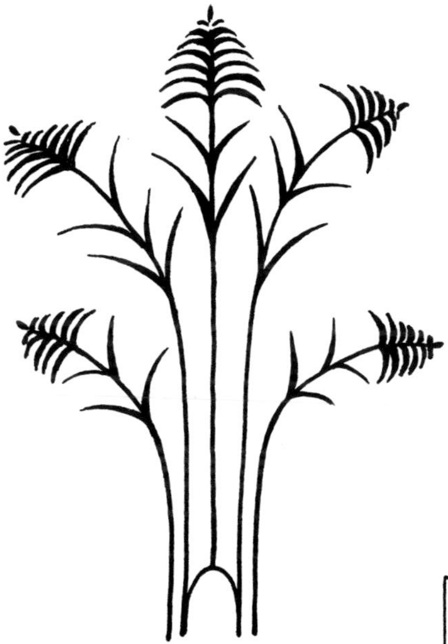

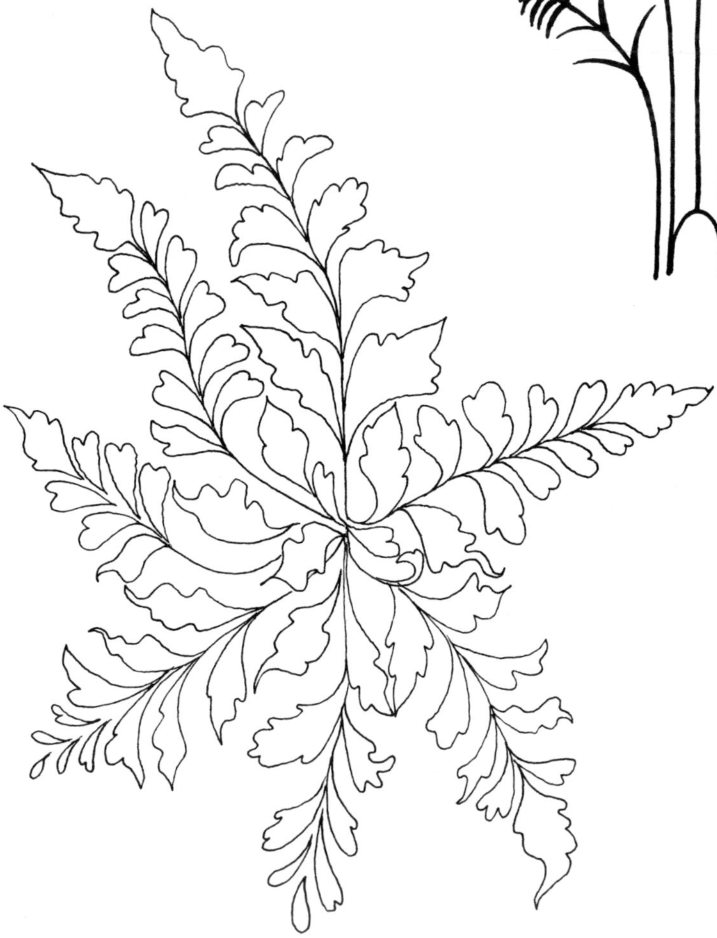

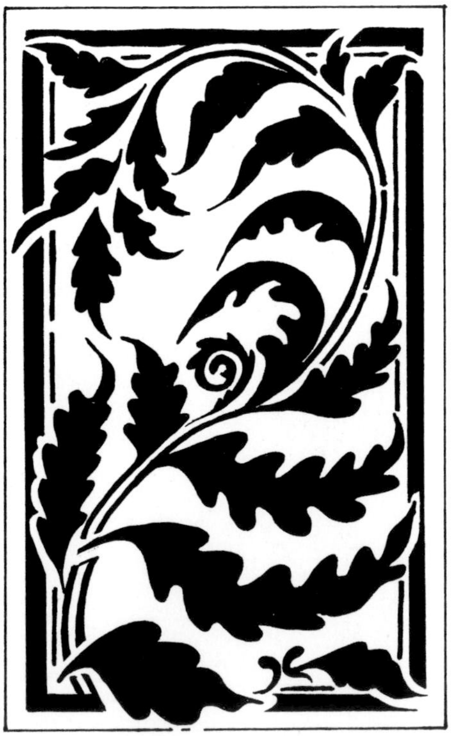

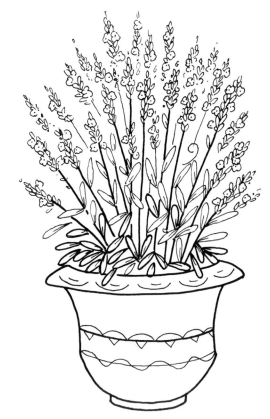

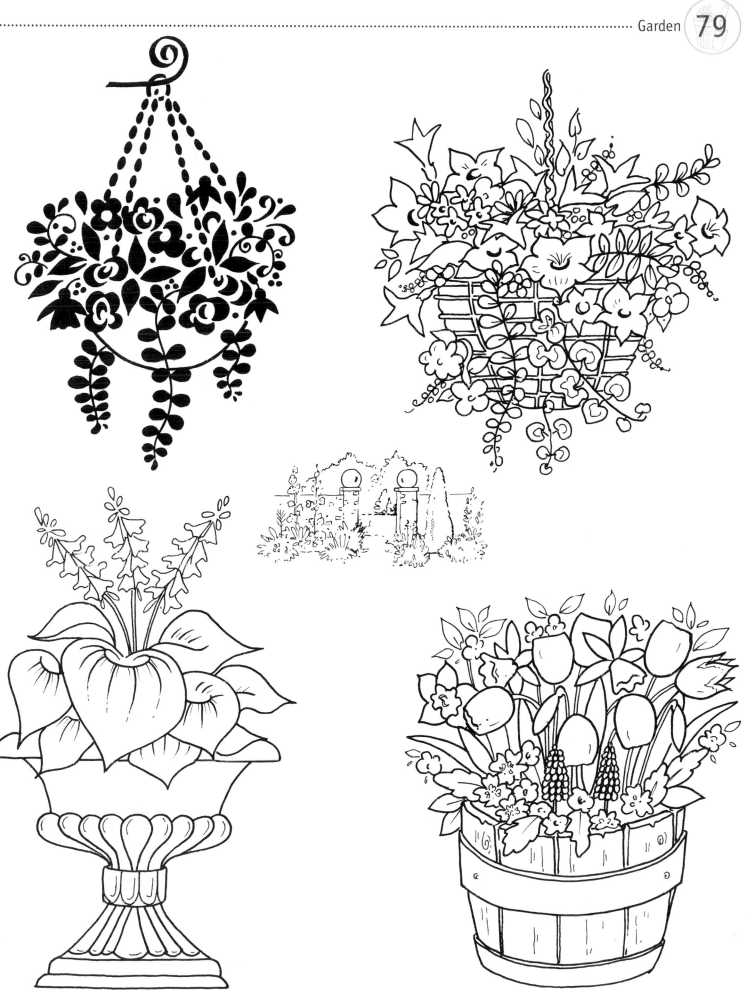

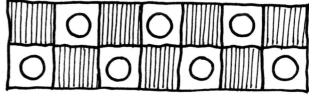

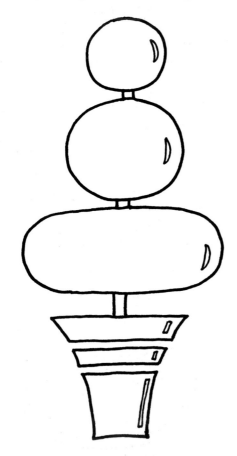

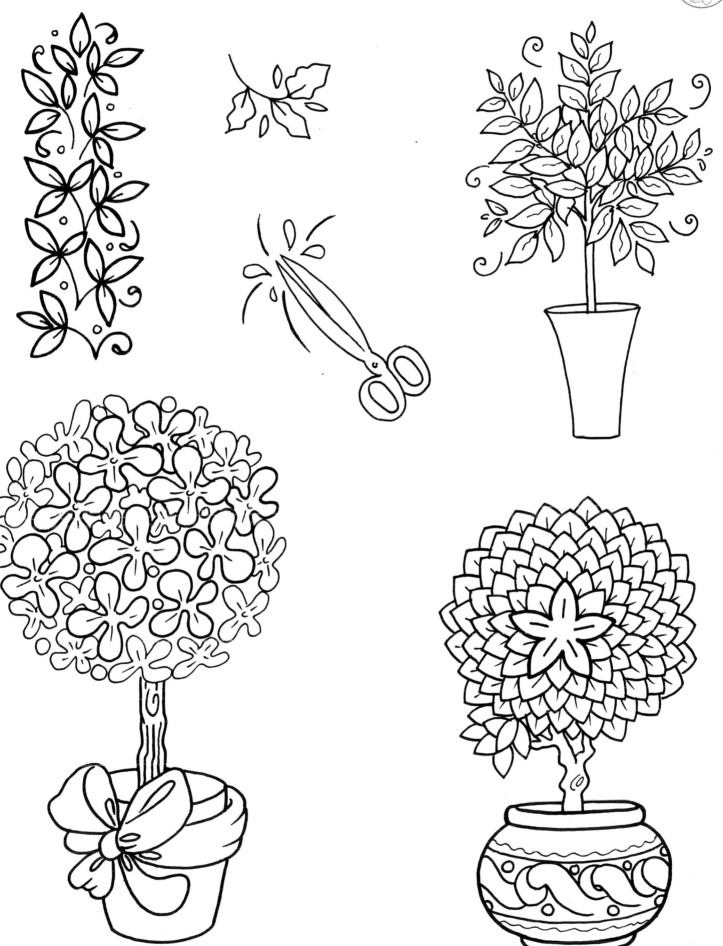

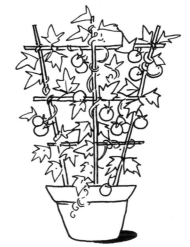

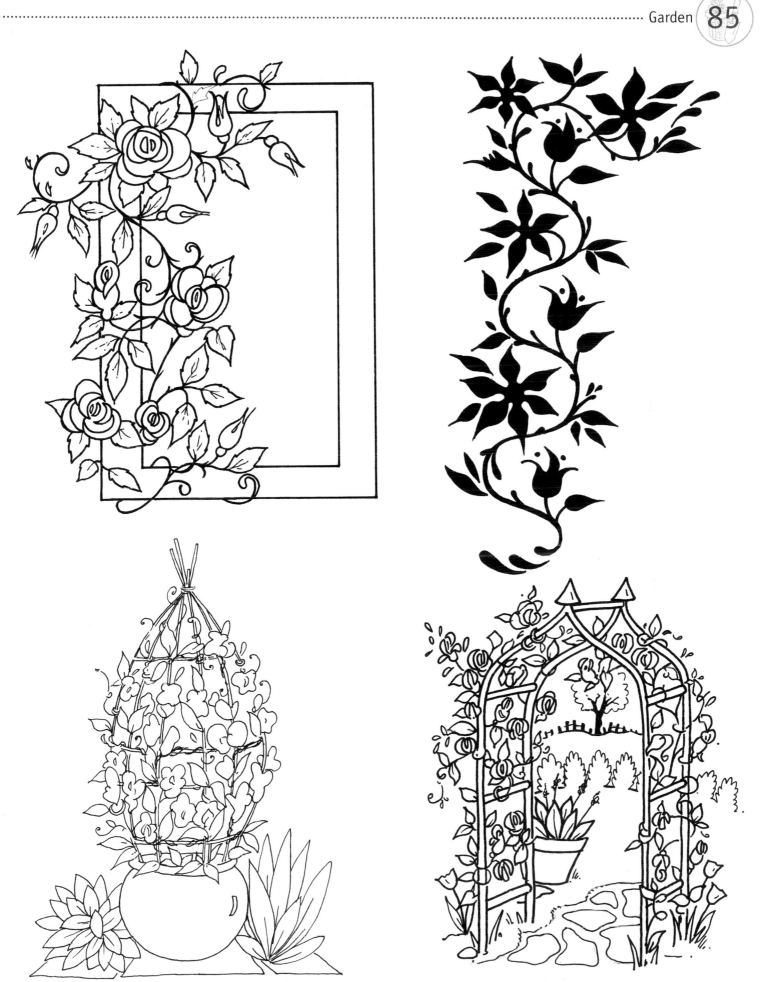

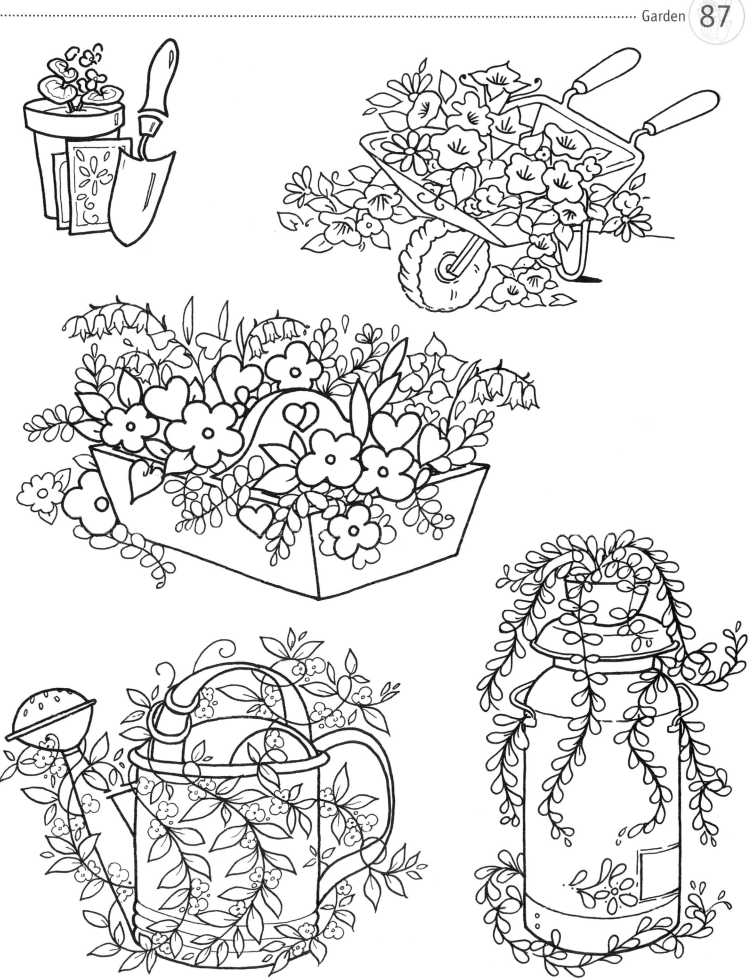

Wild and hedgerow

This useful category of floral images includes all those familiar favourites that bloom in the most unlikely places from lawns, fields and woodlands to small patches of waste ground, cracks in paving and windswept seaside areas. Some of our most popular floral images, such as poppies and daises are included in this group, their bright colours dancing merrily against a plain background of grass or corn.

Even weeds can provide us with some lovely references for crafting. Indeed there is something special, even magical, about them, perhaps because they remind us of our childhood, blowing the silvery clocks of dandelions to make a wish, picking blackberries or tiny wild strawberries. And there are other wild flowers in this category too, including the elegant bluebell and delicate primrose, so you should find much to inspire you.

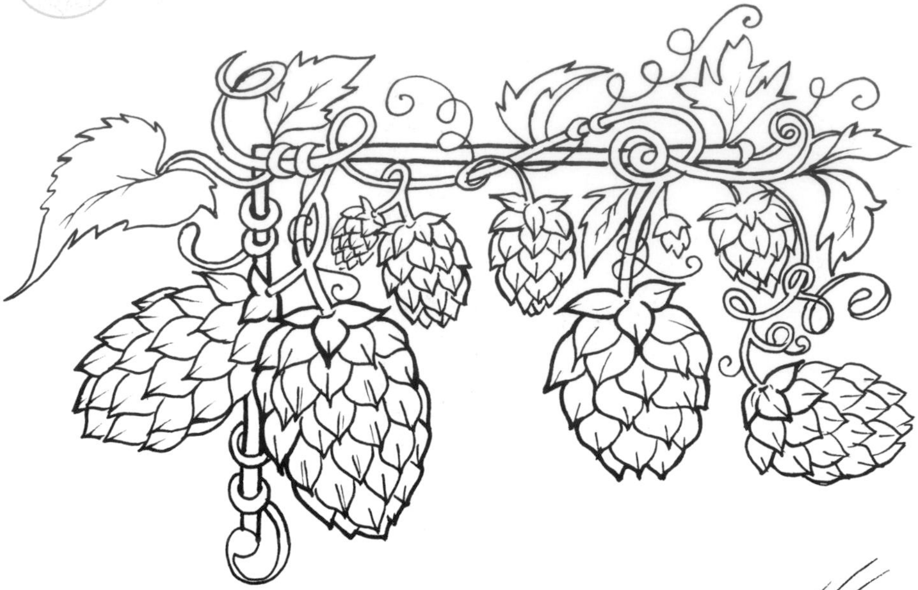

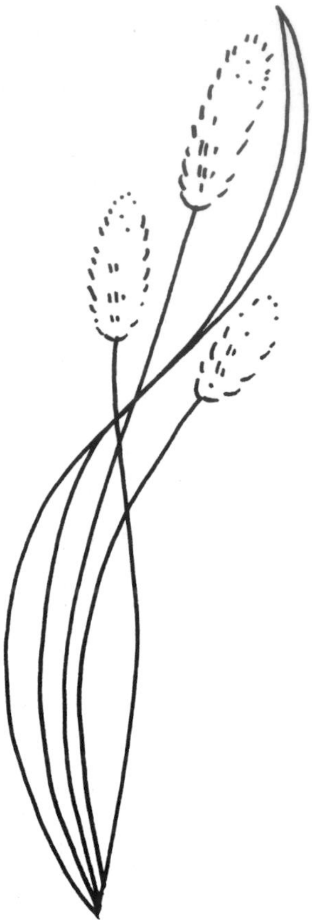

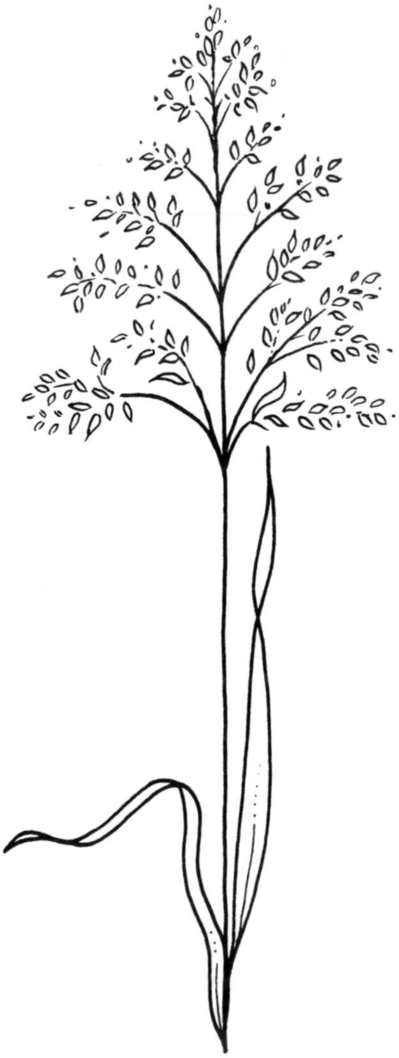

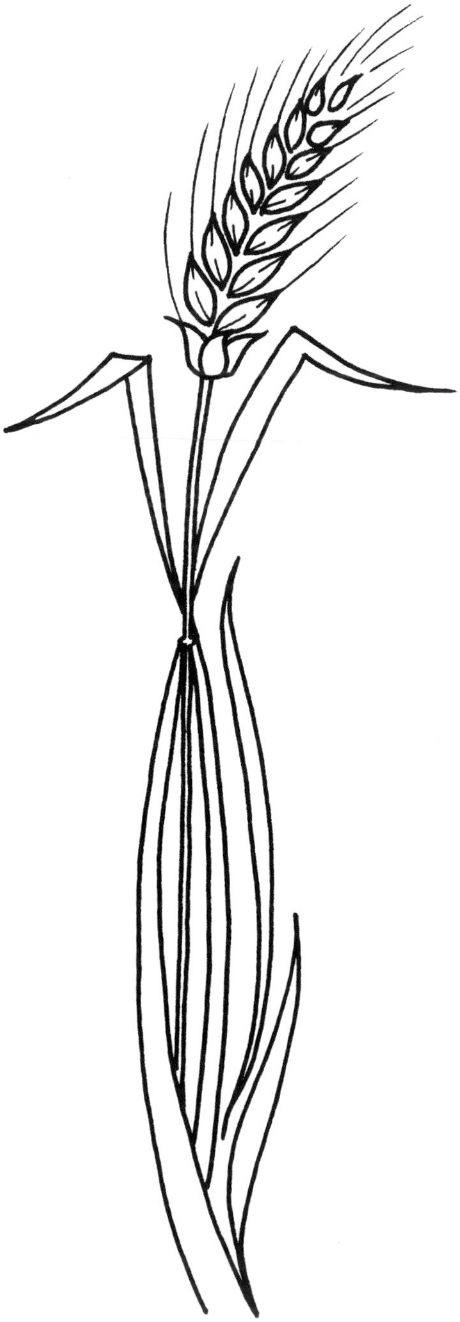

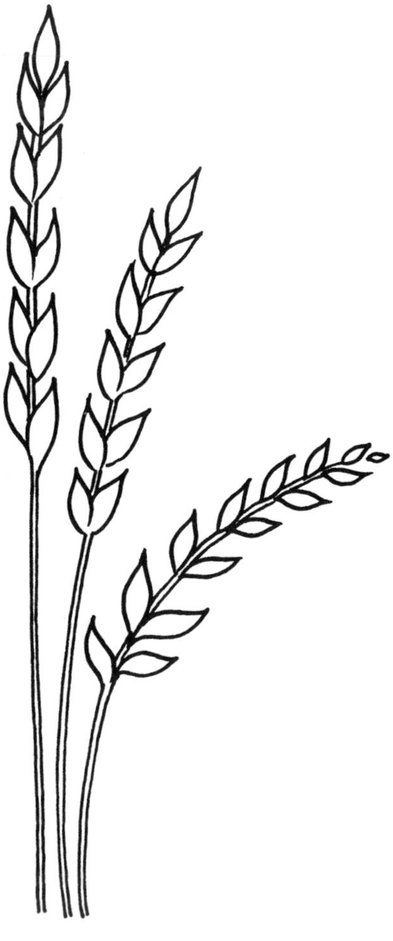

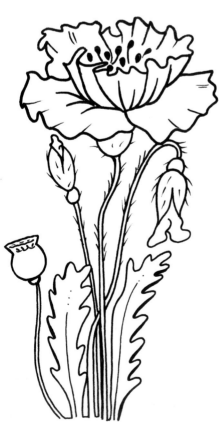

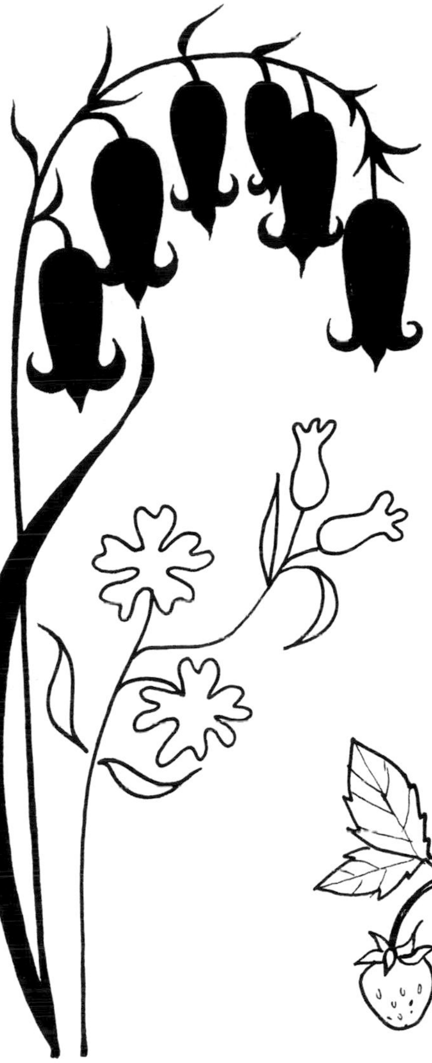

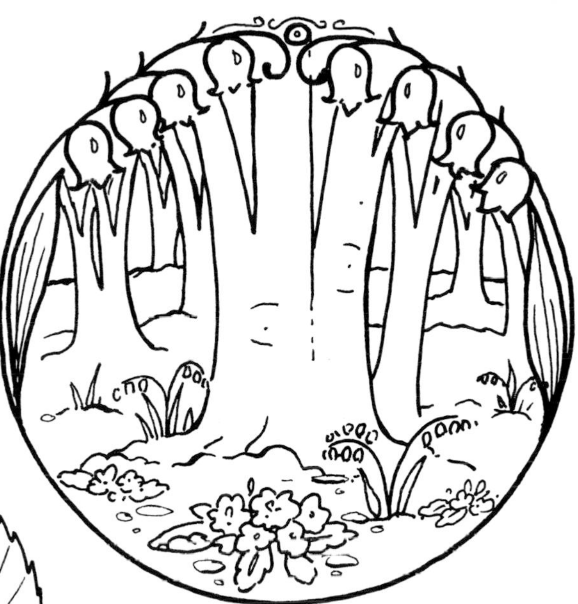

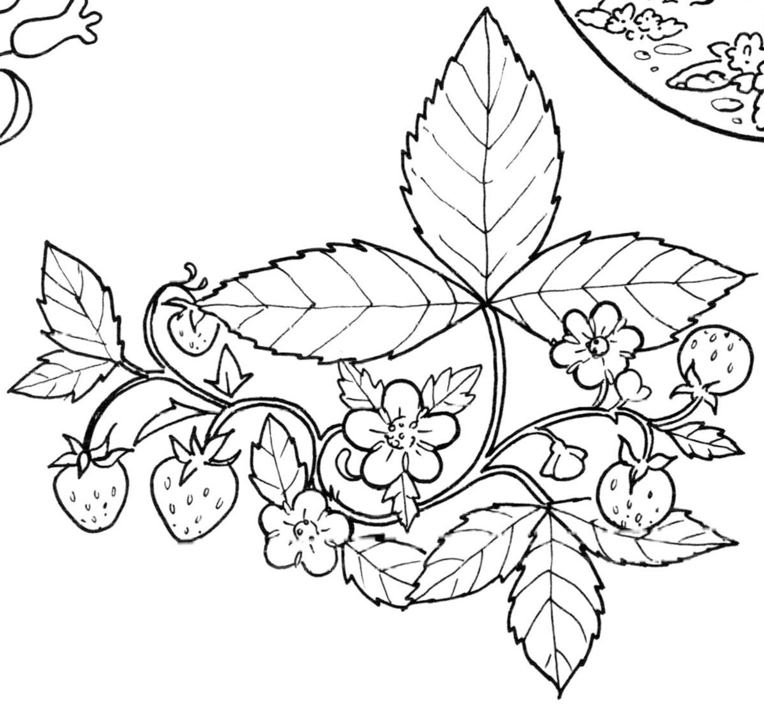

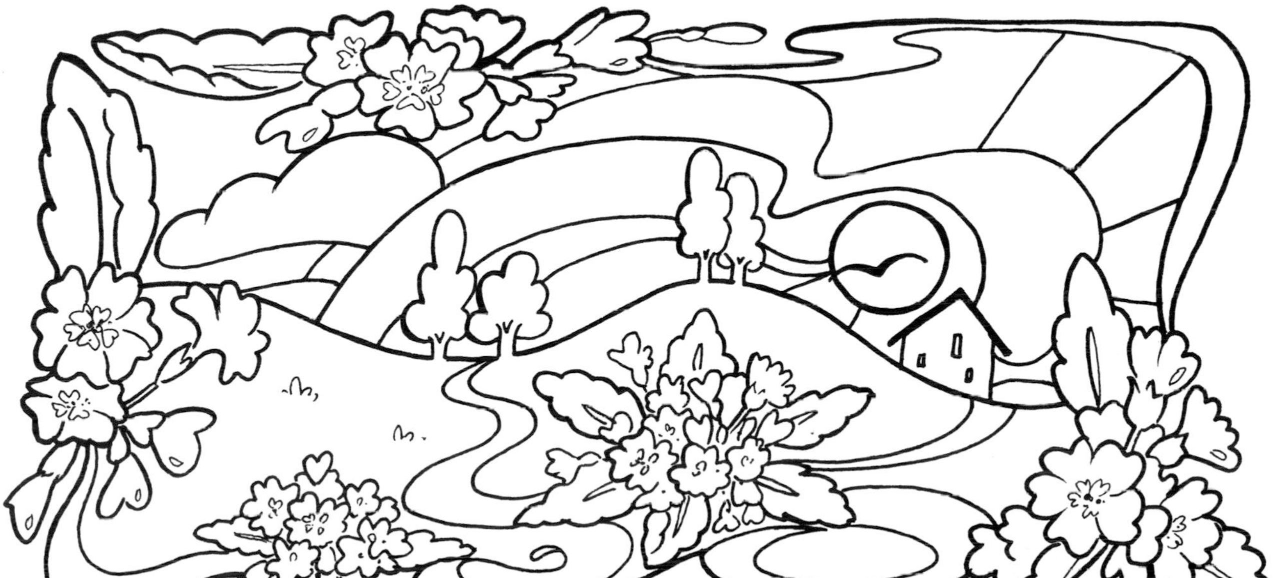

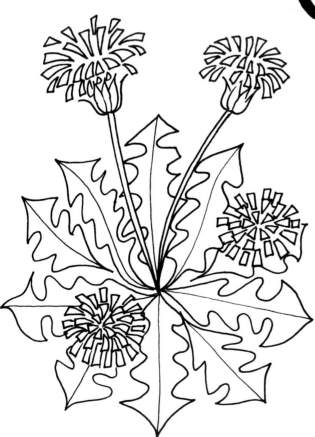

Occasions

Flowers really are suitable for all occasions, both happy and sad. We use them to convey love, sorrow and simple appreciation for a job well done or for the support of a good friend. And because it is for special occasions that we are most likely to make cards and gifts, this category really is a huge arena for crafting purposes.

These motifs are divided roughly into the categories of birth, romance, Easter, weddings general bouquets, Christmas and remembrance. However, you can adapt any of these images to extend the list much further. For example, the images on the first page could be used for a child's birthday, while the final images would be suitable for a baptism or confirmation. Remember, too, that you can use any of the other floral motifs from this book to mark a special occasion.

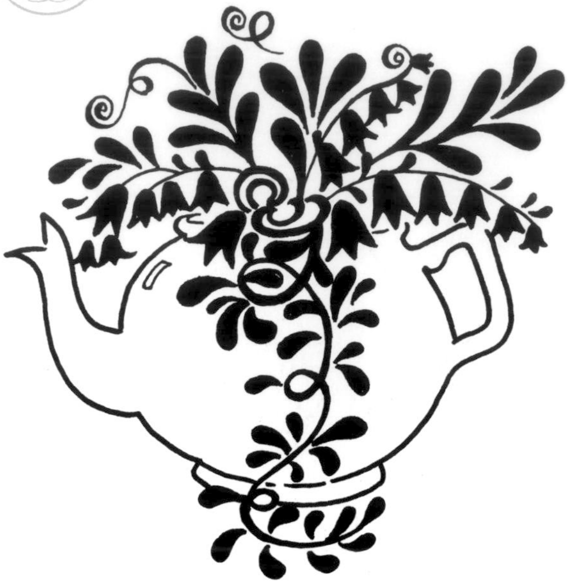

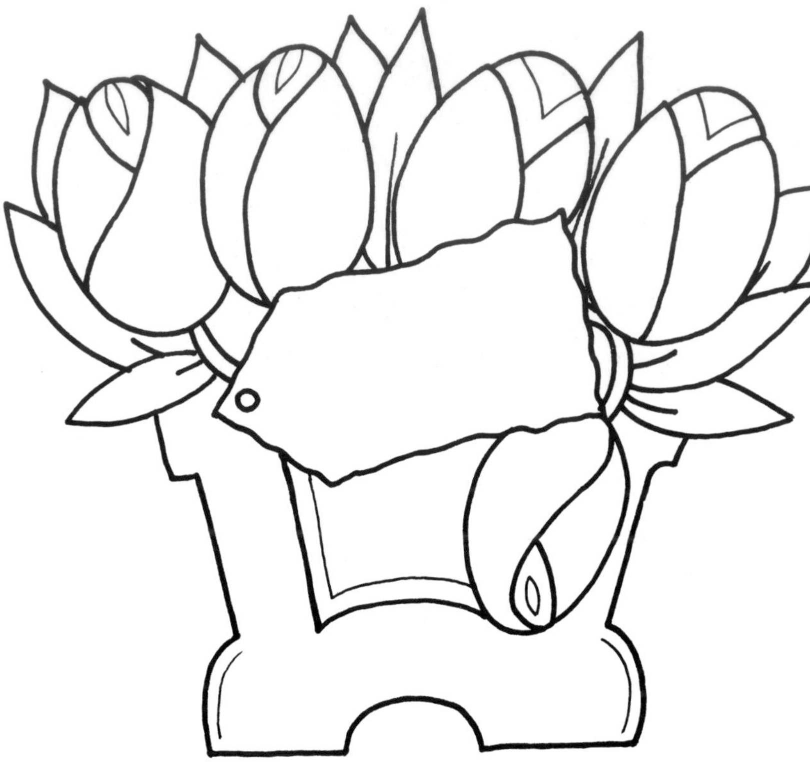

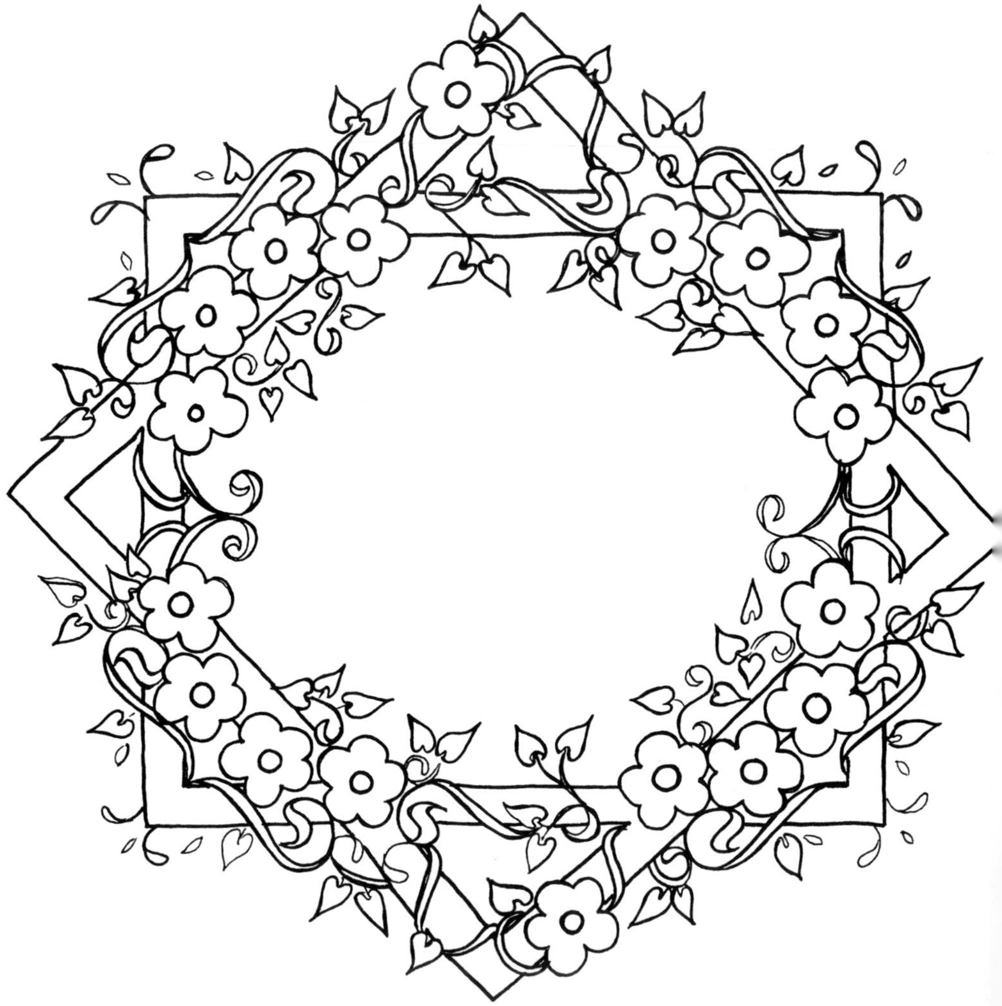

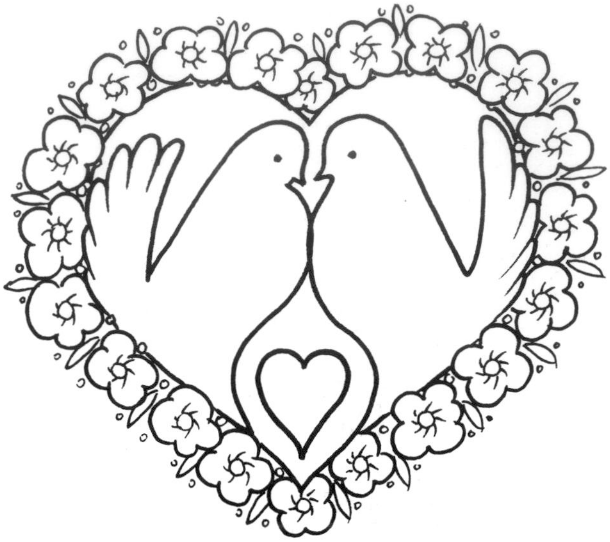

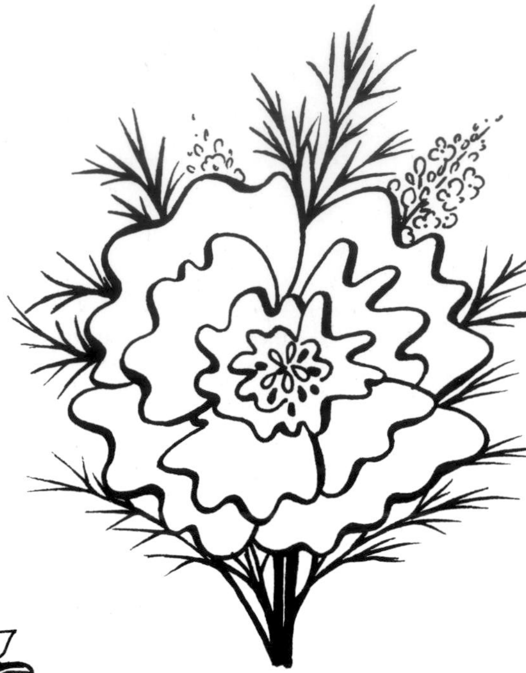

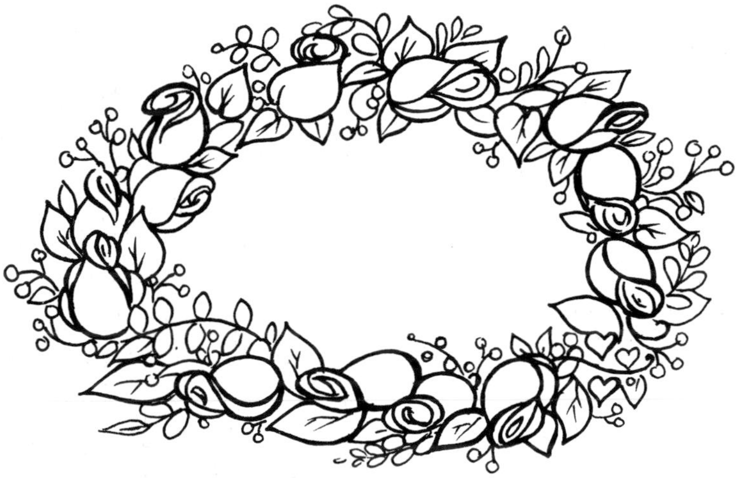

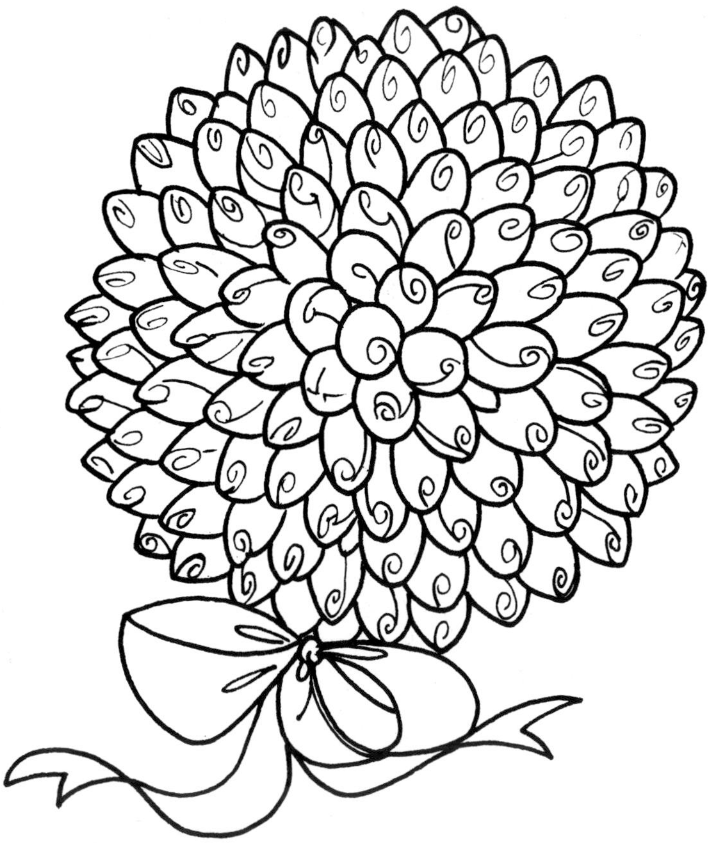

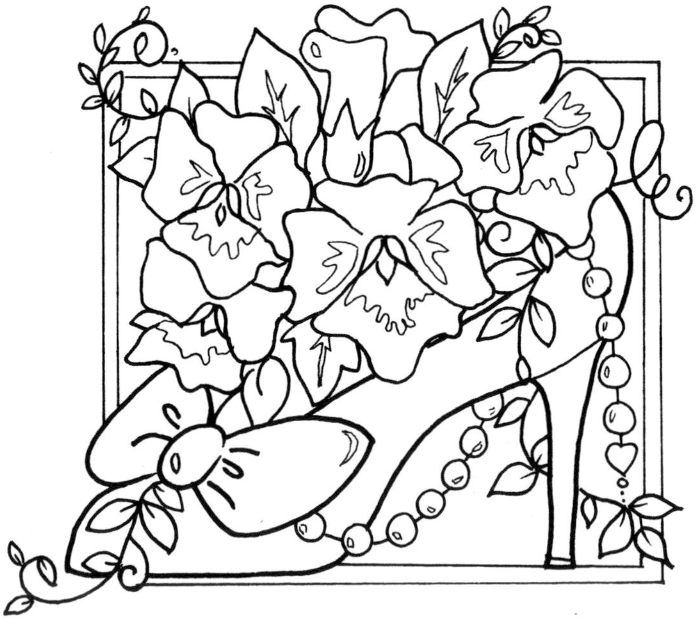

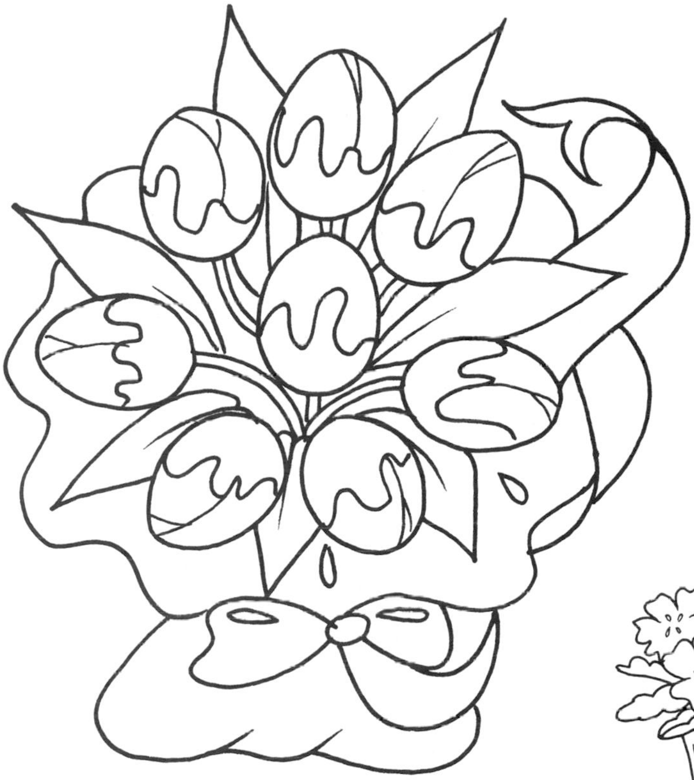

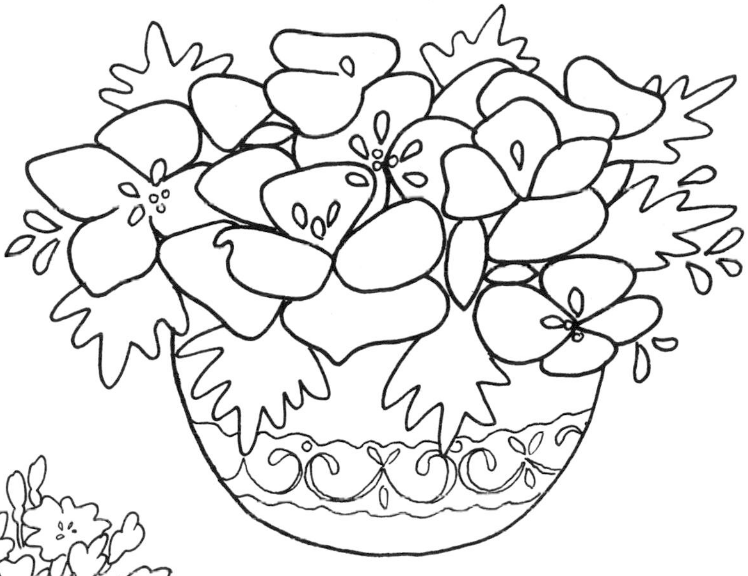

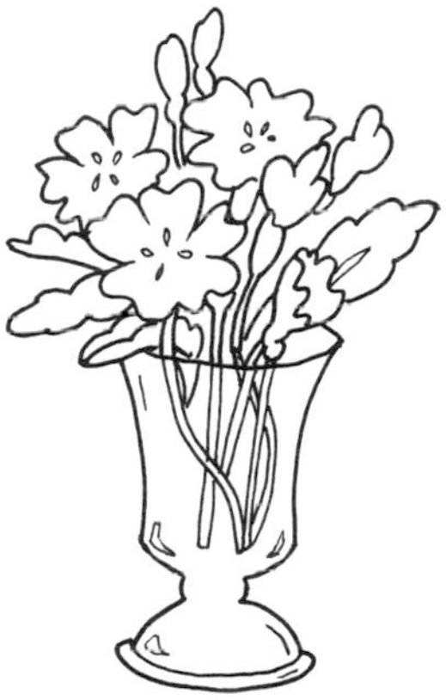

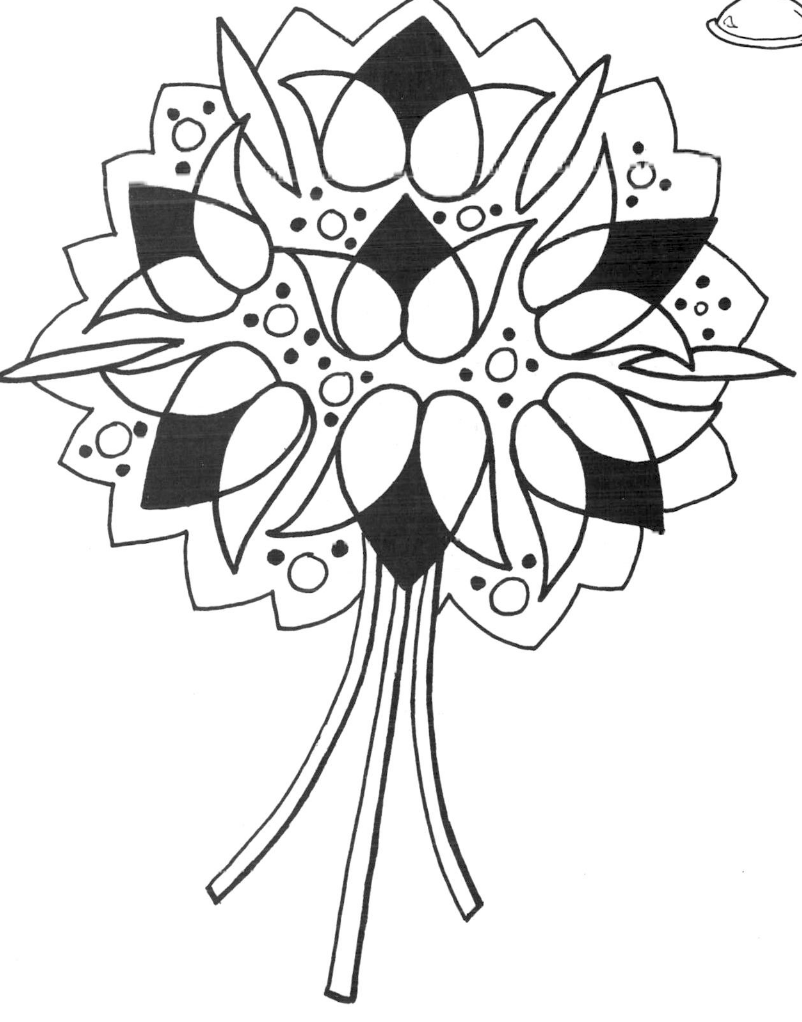

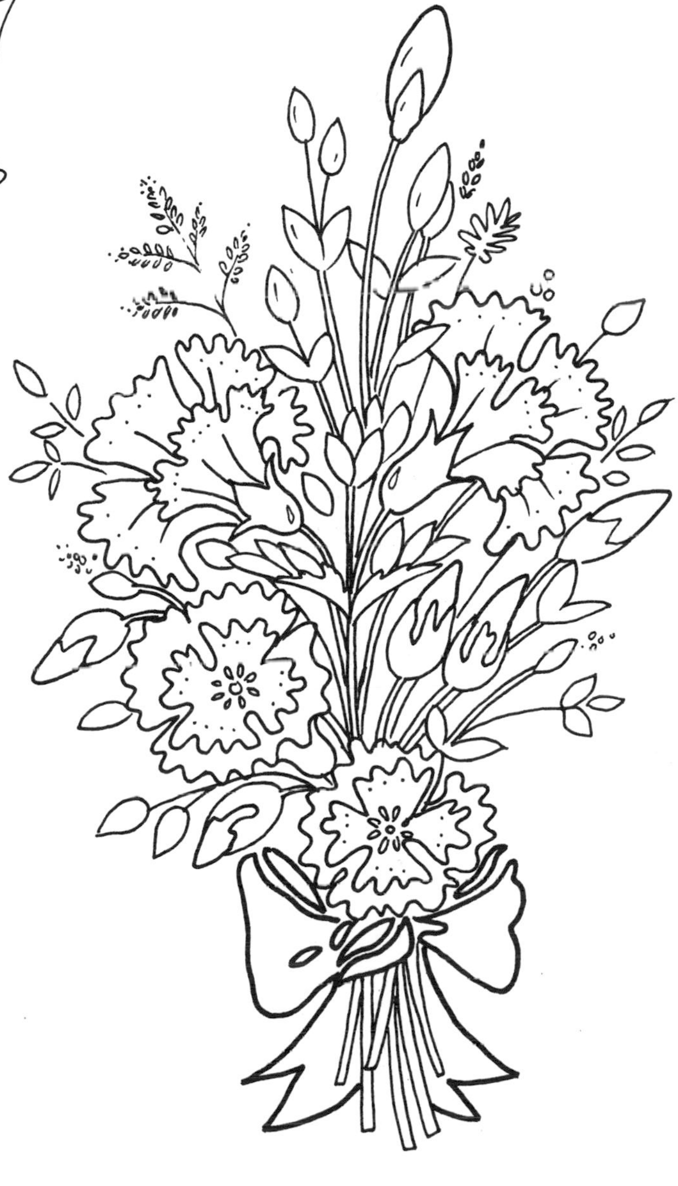

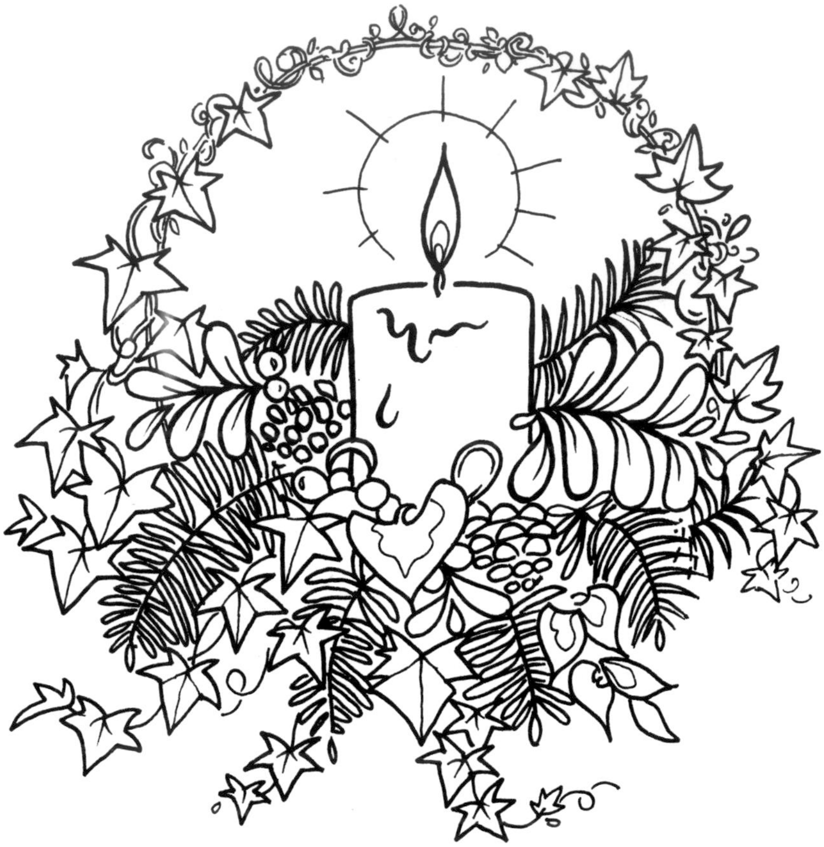

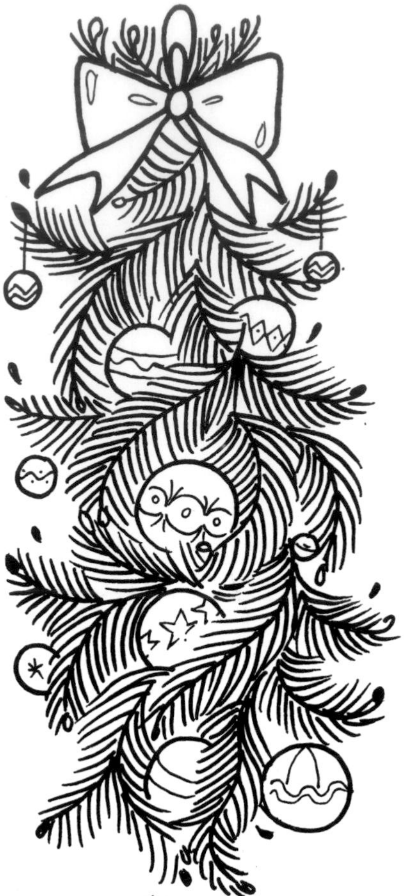

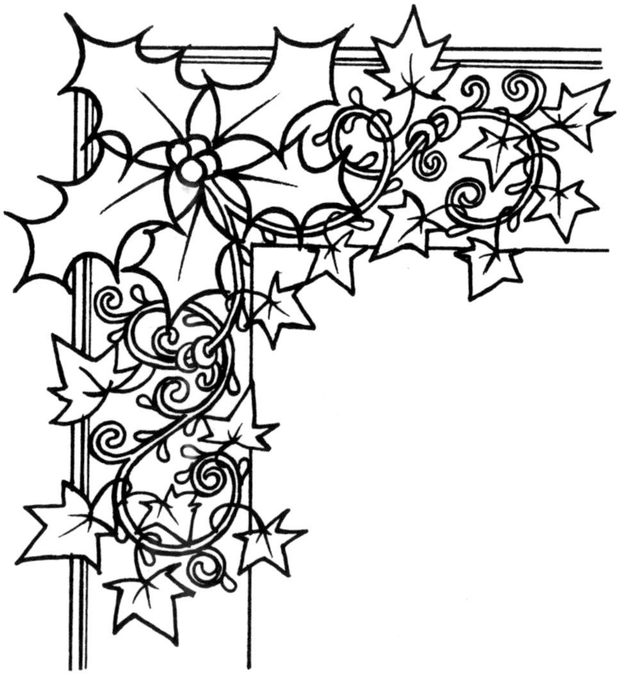

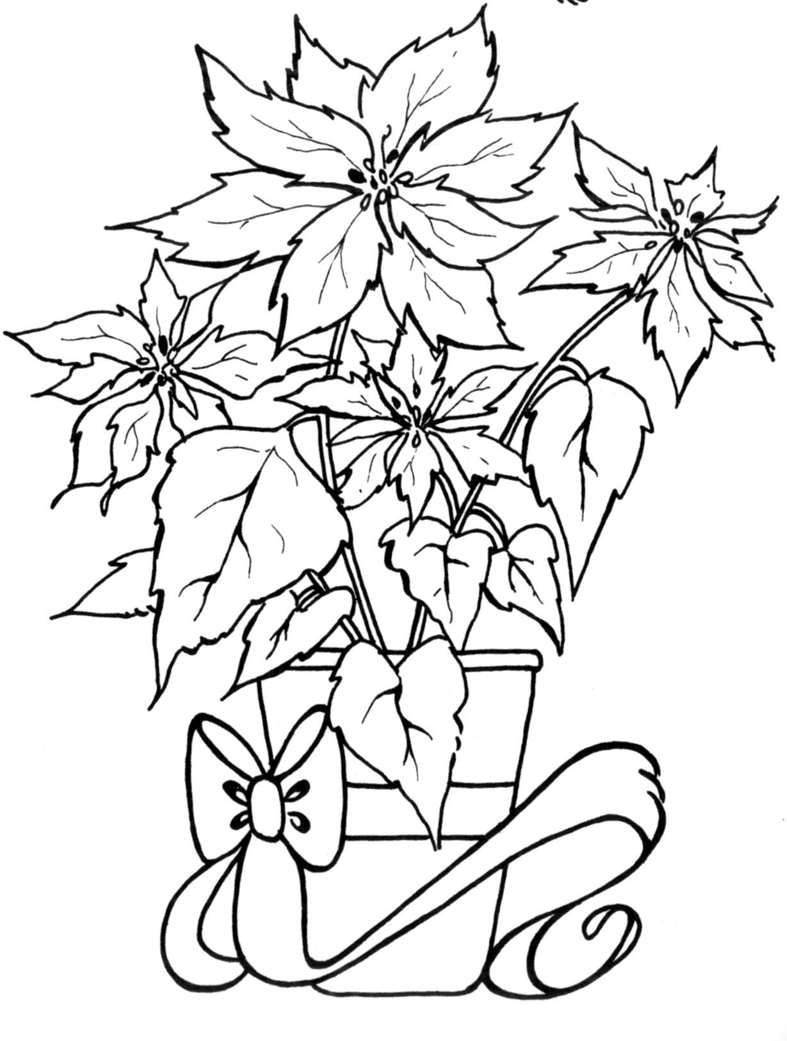

Flowers of the world

There are some images that we associate strongly with certain parts of the world – the shamrock of Ireland, the thistle of Scotland and the maple leaf of Canada, for example. These images are included here along with the lotus flowers that remind us of China and the palm trees of the Pacific islands. You'll also find cactuses, grapes, eucalyptus and lilies, which can all be used in your crafting projects to represent a particular location or simply to give your work an exotic feel.

Additionally, some motifs are drawn in a design or style that helps capture the nature of their homelands – the hibiscus is shown with a humming bird to pinpoint its tropical location, while the cherry blossom and bamboo are drawn in oriental style. You can have lots of fun trying out new techniques to suit these far-flung locations.

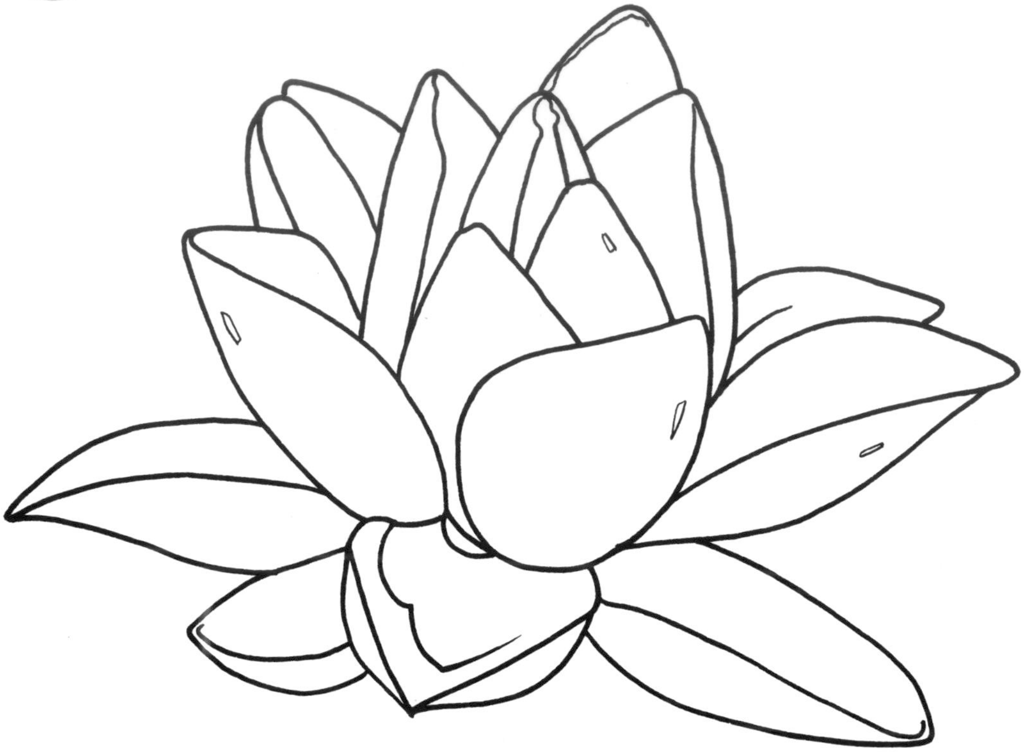
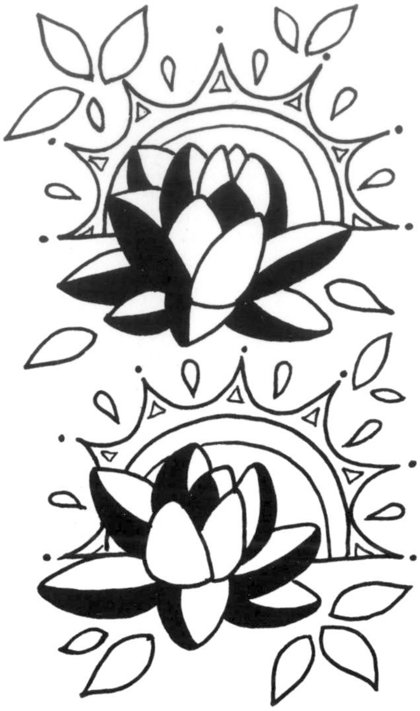
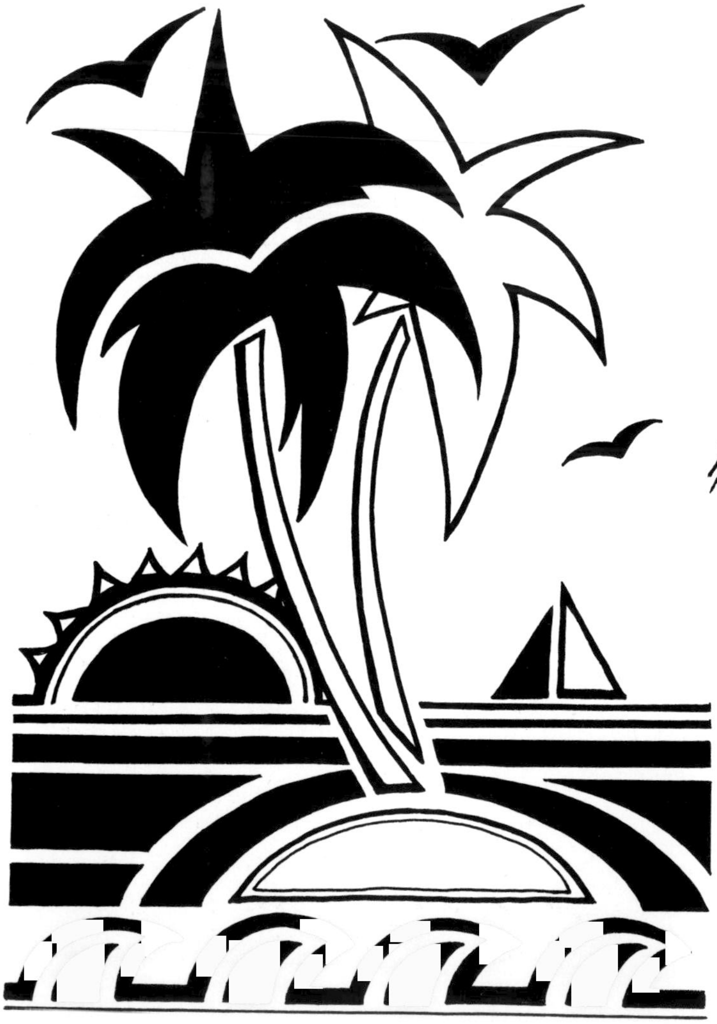
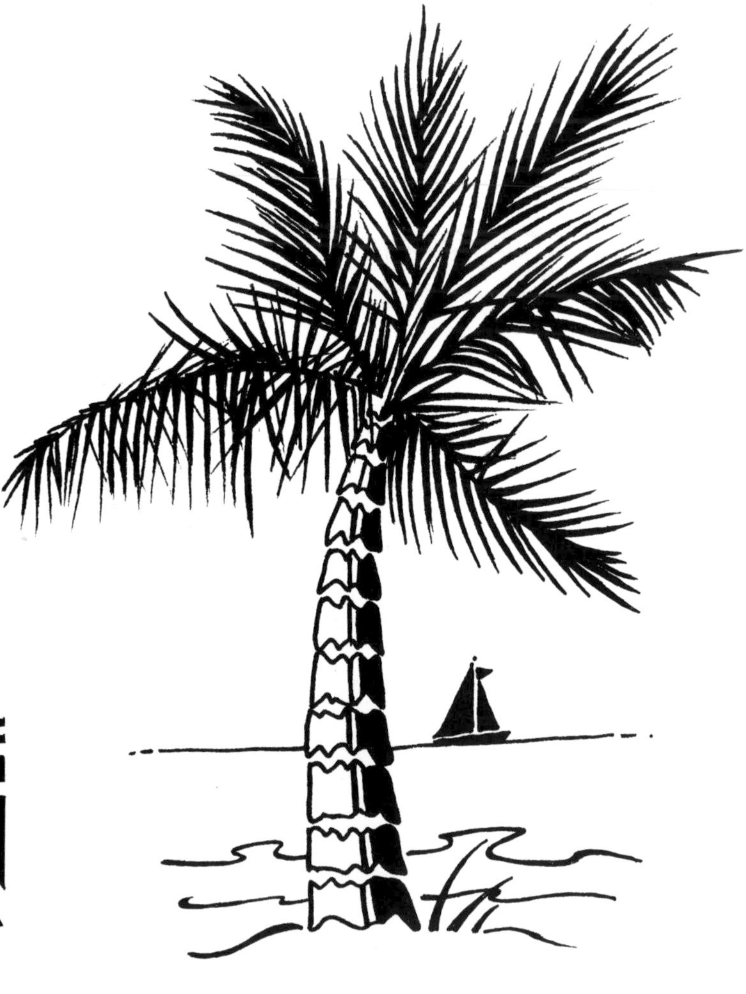

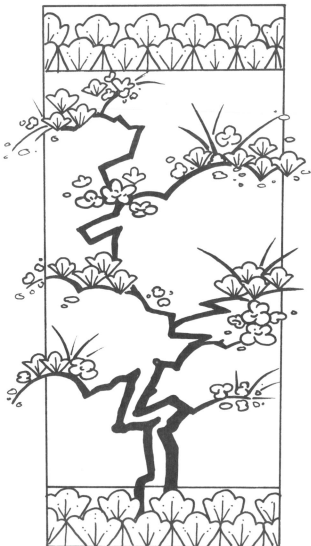

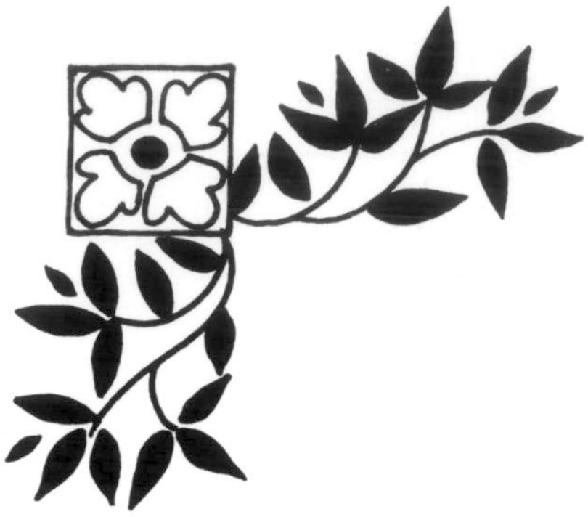

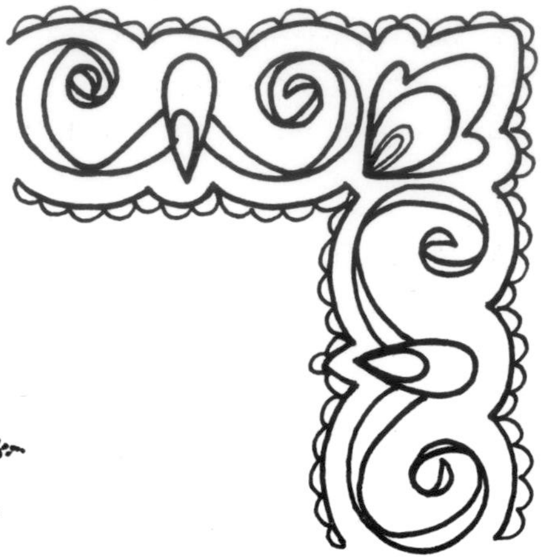

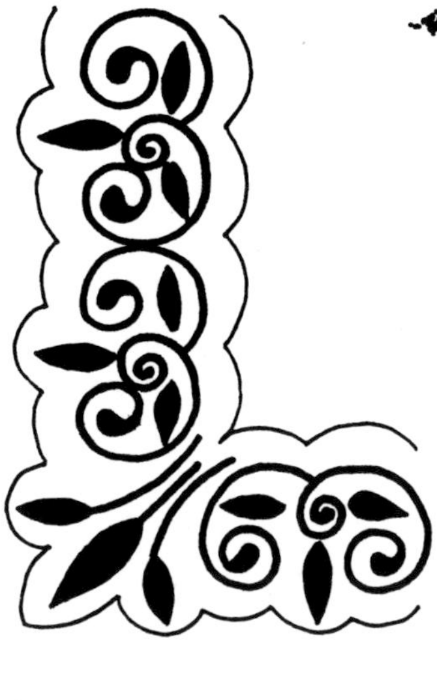

About the author

Sharon Bennett studied graphics and illustration at college before embarking upon a successful career as a packaging designer for various consultancies, eventually becoming Senior Designer for a major confectionery company. In 1986 she became freelance in order to divide her time between her work and bringing up her family. It was during this time that she moved into the craft world and began to contribute projects to national UK magazines such as *Crafts Beautiful*, and worked on their craft booklets. This is Sharon's second book, her first being *The Crafter's Design Library: Christmas*. Sharon lives with her family in Halstead, Essex, UK.

Index